Contents

C000084080

Welcome!   3

About reading the Bible   4

Section 1: Meeting Jesus

Day 1   7   The man who was just looking

Day 2   8   The woman who was looking for love

Day 3   9   The man who was looking for freedom

Section 2: 'I am a new creation'

Day 4   10   God's gift

Day 5   11   Welcome to the family!

Day 6   12   SOS

Day 7   13   Destination – heaven!

Day 8   14   How can I be sure?

Section 3: We all have a part to play

Day 9   15   Trust and obey

Day 10   16   Sin is serious

Day 11   17   I'm *really* sorry...

Day 12   18   I'm forgiven!

Day 13   19   Forgiving others

Day 14   20   New priorities

Day 15   21   Making time for God

Section 4: Building our relationship with God

Day 16   22   To God be the glory!

Day 17   23   Hallelujah! Praise the Lord!

Day 18   24   What is prayer?

Contents

Day 19	25	How do I pray?
Day 20	26	Difficulties in prayer
Day 21	27	Why read the Bible?
Day 22	28	A public proclamation
Day 23	29	Giving to God

Section 5: Power for living

Day 24	30	Becoming like Jesus
Day 25	31	Training for perfection
Day 26	32	Filled to the brim
Day 27	33	Getting better
Day 28	34	How do I know what God wants?
Day 29	35	Shining in the darkness

Section 6: Keeping going

Day 30	36	Why go to church?
Day 31	37	'I love you'
Day 32	38	A recipe for relationships
Day 33	39	What are spiritual gifts?
Day 34	40	A gift for me?
Day 35	41	Do this in remembrance of me
Day 36	42	Knowing the enemy
Day 37	43	Our defences are up!
Day 38	44	Jesus will come again
Day 39	45	He will judge the earth
Day 40	46	Keeping going

What next?	47

Welcome!

I f you have just taken the most important decision of your life and committed yourself to becoming a Christian, a follower of Jesus Christ, then this book is for you. It will introduce you to the greatest of all books, the Bible – which is not only the guide and handbook for our Christian journey, but is also where we will meet with God – and it will explain and illustrate the basics of the Christian faith.

But perhaps you have not yet taken the decision to become a Christian. Perhaps you want to know a bit more of what Christianity is all about, to be absolutely sure before you take such a big step. This book will be helpful for you, too. Read the Bible passages carefully and, with the help of the notes, think about what they are showing you about the Christian faith. Then when you are sure you are ready to make a commitment to becoming a Christian, you might like to use the following prayer:

'Dear loving Father, I am sorry for all the wrong things I have done, and for going my way instead of yours. Thank you that Jesus died for me, and that my sins are now forgiven. I now commit myself wholly to you, and ask that Jesus will take charge of my life as my Lord and Saviour.' Or maybe you have been a churchgoer for many years, but have always felt there was 'something more' that you had never quite got hold of? Then this book will be helpful for you too. As you read the passages, which may be familiar to you, try to imagine that this is the first time you have heard them. Listen to God's voice speaking, personally, to you. At some point you may feel ready to use the following prayer:

'Dear loving Father, today I recommit my life to you I am sorry for any half-heartedness and lack of sincerity in my love for you. Thank you that in Jesus I can see the fullness of your love for me. I give you now, in total completeness, my life and my love.'

Whatever your situation, my own prayer is that you will find joy, delight, instruction and challenge in the words of the Bible.

Writer **Gillian Peall**
Gillian is one of Scripture Union's regular writers for *Daily Bread*. Before moving to Cheshire with her husband to be nearer to her two young grandsons, she worked on the nursing staff of her local hospital for the elderly. Now she visits local nursing homes regularly just to chat with the patients there. She attends her local Christian Life Fellowship, and has a special interest in helping new Christians grow in their faith.

About reading the Bible

Before you begin

To get the most out of reading the Bible, you will need to use a good modern translation. This book follows the New International Version – but can be used with any Bible version. Other popular versions include the Contemporary English Version (CEV), the Good News Bible (GNB), the New English Bible (NEB), the New Living Translation (NLT) and the Revised Standard Version (RSV). The old King James, or Authorised, Version (AV) is still a classic expression of the English language, like Shakespeare's plays, but more accurate translations can be made today because of our improved understanding of the original languages; and, also like Shakespeare's plays, the AV language is very different from the English we speak today, and can be quite difficult to understand.

About the Bible

Taken as a whole, the Bible looks very formidable! But it is really a whole library of books, rather than just one book, written by many authors over a period of around 1,500 years. It contains history, biography, theology, poetry and philosophy: Christians believe that all of the Bible is inspired by God, and that God reveals himself to us through the Bible.

First the Bible traces the history of God's chosen people, the Jews, until eventually Jesus, the Son of God, comes to us on earth. It then goes on to tell us about Jesus' ministry here on earth, and the growth of the Christian church.

Everything in each one of these books is God's word to us. As the apostle Paul says, 'All Scripture is God-breathed and is useful for teaching, rebuking, correcting and training in righteousness, so that the man of God may be thoroughly equipped for every good work.'

The books of the Bible

The Old Testament consists of books written before the birth of Jesus. It begins with the five great books of history and law, sometimes known as the Pentateuch. The story of the Jewish nation follows in the twelve books of history and biography from Joshua to Esther. These books are followed by five books of poetry and wisdom writing from Job to the Song of Songs. These in turn are followed by the writings, words and visions of the prophets, in 17 books from Isaiah to Malachi. The New Testament consists of the four Gospels (which tell the story of the life and ministry of Jesus), Acts ('The Acts of the Apostles', to give its full title, where we read of the beginnings of the early church), letters of Paul and other disciples, and finally the visionary book of Revelation.

Finding your way around

Particular parts of the Bible are pinpointed by the name of the book, followed by the chapter number, followed by the verse – this is known as the Bible reference. Paul's words which I quoted earlier ('All Scripture is ...') are found in his second letter to Timothy, chapter 3, verses 16 and 17 and the Bible reference is written as 2 Timothy 3:16,17. Quite often the book names are abbreviated, so our reference might appear as 2 Tim 3:16,17.

In the front of your Bible will be an index or contents page showing you where to find each book. It might seem a bit daunting, but you will soon start to know your way around!

Using Bible reading notes

Most Bible reading notes cover all or part of a book over a period of several days. Because the notes you are using now are designed specially for new believers, and so cover a wide range of subjects, you will find they jump around the Bible a bit!

What should you do when you settle down to read the Bible with the help of Bible reading notes? Here's one possible approach to reading these notes. Begin by being quiet; focus on God, and put other thoughts out of your mind. Then ask God to help you understand what you will be reading; you could say something like, 'Dear Heavenly Father, please speak to me as I read your Word, and help me understand and respond to what you say.' Reading the little introduction to the note should also help you to prepare for reading the Bible. Then find the appropriate passage in your Bible, and read it slowly and carefully. Think about the Bible passage; ask yourself, 'What is God saying to me?' Then read the rest of the note; it may help you to understand the passage and its message better, and it may point you to other things to pray about, think about or do. The final paragraph of the note will help you to respond to what you have read, often by suggesting something to pray or think about. You may find you want to read the passage again; don't worry if you don't feel you understand everything it's saying.

But take your time: reading the Bible is the usual way God speaks to us, and we need to give ourselves space to hear his voice.

Daily Bread for New Christians will give you a good introduction to the basics of Christianity. I can guarantee, however, that it won't cover every topic and answer every question you might be thinking of – it's only 48 pages long, remember! It's important to pray for God's help in your Christian life – and to remember that one of the ways God answers such prayers is through other Christians. Talking to Christian friends c leaders in your church, listening to talks in church or on tape, reading Christian magazines and books, or watching a Christian video, are all ways God uses to speak to us. In this way, he can help us all, however long we've been Christians to know and love him more and more.

I pray that you will look forward eagerly to your daily readings, and continue with a disciplined reading plan – not as an onerous duty to be 'done' before (or after) the real business of the day, but both as a delight and as the real business of the day.

And now on to *Day 1*...

Day 1

The man who was just looking

PREPARE How did you feel when you first came face to face with Jesus? What difference has e made in your life? Over the next three days we will read the stories of three people who 1et Jesus, and the difference he made in their lives. Did you feel curious when you first heard bout the real Jesus – the man behind the familiar face? Perhaps you wanted to find out a bit 1ore, without actually committing yourself to anything. A man in Jericho felt like that.

Luke 19:1–10

esus entered Jericho and was passing 1rough. ² A man was there by the name f Zacchaeus; he was a chief tax collector nd was wealthy. ³ He wanted to see who esus was, but being a short man he could 1ot, because of the crowd. ⁴ So he ran 1head and climbed a sycamore-fig tree to ee him, since Jesus was coming that way. ⁵ When Jesus reached the spot, he looked 1p and said to him, "Zacchaeus, come 1own immediately. I must stay at your 1ouse today." ⁶ So he came down at once nd welcomed him gladly.

All the people saw this and began to 1utter, "He has gone to be the guest of a sinner'."

⁸ But Zacchaeus stood up and said to the _ord, "Look, Lord! Here and now I give 1alf of my possessions to the poor, and if I 1ave cheated anybody out of anything, I vill pay back four times the amount."

⁹ Jesus said to him, "Today salvation has ome to this house, because this man, too, s a son of Abraham. ¹⁰ For the Son of Man ame to seek and to save what was lost."

EXPLORE Zacchaeus had heard about Jesus – all of Jericho was buzzing with talk about him (v 3). But he probably also wanted to keep clear of the crowd – as a tax collector for the occupying Roman forces, he was an unpopular man! He climbed up a tree, where he could get a good view without having to force his way through an unfriendly crowd. But Jesus looks at him, and his world turns upside down. Jesus actually wants to come to *his* house! In one brief encounter and a few words, Zacchaeus's life has been fundamentally changed, and his values totally reversed (v 8). Maybe he didn't stop being a tax collector, but became that rarest of beings in those days: an honest tax collector. It's important that his reaction to Jesus was not only to put right the wrong he had done, but to 'go public'. He could have quietly restored the money he had extorted from the Jews, but he makes his decision public (v 8).

What is our reaction when we meet Jesus? Do our ideas somersault? Do we realise we will have to rethink our principles and priorities, and perhaps act to put things right? Maybe we suddenly realise this, or perhaps it grows on us gradually.

RESPOND Think about this: Jesus wants to come to your house today. How will you welcome him?

Day 2

The woman who was looking for love

John 4:1–30,39–42

... ⁷ When a Samaritan woman came to draw water, Jesus said to her, "Will you give me a drink?" ...⁹ The Samaritan woman said to him, "You are a Jew and I am a Samaritan woman. How can you ask me for a drink?" (For Jews do not associate with Samaritans.) ...

¹¹ "Sir," the woman said ... ¹² "Are you greater than our father Jacob ... ?"

¹³ Jesus answered, "Everyone who drinks this water will be thirsty again, ¹⁴ but whoever drinks the water I give him will never thirst. Indeed, the water I give him will become in him a spring of water welling up to eternal life."

¹⁵ The woman said to him, "Sir, give me this water ... "

¹⁶ He told her, "Go, call your husband and come back."

¹⁷ "I have no husband," she replied. Jesus said to her, "... ¹⁸ The fact is, you have had five husbands, and the man you now have is not your husband. ..."

¹⁹ "Sir," the woman said, "I can see that you are a prophet ..."

²¹ Jesus declared, "Believe me, woman, a time is coming when you will worship the Father neither on this mountain nor in Jerusalem. ... ²³ the true worshippers will worship the Father in spirit and truth, for they are the kind of worshippers the Father seeks. ²⁴ God is spirit, and his worshippers must worship in spirit and in truth."

²⁵ The woman said, "I know that Messiah" (called Christ) "is coming. When he comes, he will explain everything to us."

²⁶ Then Jesus declared, "I who speak to you am he." ...

EXPLORE **It was not the done thing for
Jesus to ask a Samaritan woman for a
drink, but then Jesus never has been
interested in 'the done thing'! The
woman's lifestyle would have been
considered immoral. Jesus knew that sh[e
was an outcast, shunned by the other
village women, preferring to collect he[r
water in the heat of midday and avoid
the evening gossip around the well.
Maybe she sought love, security and
affection from her husbands and
partners. But Jesus challenges her by h[er
extraordinary request. Knowing how a[
male Jew would normally treat her, sh[e
taken aback (v 9). But Jesus knows all
about this woman (vs 17,18,29), and
offers her the eternal hope and love th[at
she needs (vs 13,14,23,24).**

**What is *our* reaction to Jesus' offer? [The
woman tries to sidestep it with 'religio[us
red herrings (vs 19,20,25). But when sh[e
grasps what Jesus says (v 26), what do[es
she do? She rushes to the village and
conveys her excitement to the other fo[lk
despite what they think of her. They g[o
to see this amazing man, who seems t[o
know all about the woman; they, in th[eir
turn, meet Jesus and listen, accepting t[he
truth (v 41). Can we share our
excitement about Jesus, even to those
who are prejudiced against us or Jesus.[**

Day 3

The man who was looking for freedom

PREPARE Has your life ever been in such a mess that you gave in to despair, and just 'wanted out'? Or maybe you know someone like that; perhaps someone controlled and driven by ravings and addictions such as drink, drugs, money, status or gambling?

Luke 8:26–39

26 They sailed to the region of the Gerasenes ... 27 Jesus ... was met by a demon-possessed man ... For a long time this man had not worn clothes or lived in a house, but had lived in the tombs. 28 When he saw Jesus, he cried out and fell at his feet, shouting at the top of his voice, "What do you want with me, Jesus, Son of the Most High God? I beg you, don't torture me!" 29 For Jesus had commanded the evil spirit to come out of the man. ... Though he was chained ... and kept under guard, he had broken his chains and had been driven ... into solitary places.

30 Jesus asked him, "What is your name?" "Legion," he replied, because many demons had gone into him. 31 And they begged him repeatedly not to order them to go into the Abyss.

32 A ... herd of pigs was ... on the hillside. The demons begged Jesus to let them go into them, and he gave them permission. 33 When the demons came out of the man, they went into the pigs, and the herd rushed ... into the lake and was drowned. 34 When those tending the pigs saw what had happened, they ran off and reported this ... 35 and the people went out to see ... When they came to Jesus, they found the man ... sitting at Jesus' feet, dressed and in his right mind; and they were afraid. ... 37 Then all the people of the region of the Gerasenes asked Jesus to leave them, because they were overcome with fear. So he got into the boat and left.

39 ... the man went away and told all over the town how much Jesus had done for him.

EXPLORE The demons possessing this man are very real. They recognise the authority Jesus has to send them to the Abyss (vs 28,31 – a place of imprisonment). Jesus knows how desperately the man needs release from the power of those demons, and simply commands them to go (vs 29,33). The effect is awe-inspiring and frightening (vs 33,35). The man who had been unable to live normally (v 27) was now sitting quietly, fully dressed and talking to this incredible man, Jesus! Such a demonstration of authority over evil can terrify those who see it without understanding who Jesus is. Jesus' authority is still there today, for those who need release from those addictions which are driving them to destruction. Sadly, not everyone sees Jesus as the answer (v 37).

The man begs to join the disciples (v 38). Why not? He had a wonderful story of release him from his desperate situation. Rejected by his family and friends – why stay? But Jesus says, 'No; go home and tell what God has done for you' (v 39). Going to a foreign land as a missionary may sometimes seem an exciting way of serving Jesus, but Jesus often asks us to stay where we are to tell our family, friends and neighbours the good news.

RESPOND Pray something like this: 'Thank you, Lord, that you accept us whatever we are like.'

Day 4

God's gift

PREPARE 'If anyone is in Christ, he is a new creation; the old has gone, the new has come!'
(2 Corinthians 5:17). Over the next five days we will find out what it means to be a new
person, to be 'born again'.
   Have you ever received a gift that you thought you didn't deserve? How did you feel?
Embarrassed, or overwhelmed by the kindness, or perhaps guilty that you hadn't done
anything to deserve it? God offers a gift to all of us, with no strings attached. What is it? H
do we receive it? Today's passage is from one of the letters that Paul wrote to new churche
Before you open your Bible, ask God to help you understand what you read.

Ephesians 2:1–10

As for you, you were dead in your
transgressions and sins, ² in which you
used to live when you followed the ways of
this world and of the ruler of the kingdom
of the air, the spirit who is now at work in
those who are disobedient. ³ All of us also
lived among them at one time, gratifying
the cravings of our sinful nature and
following its desires and thoughts. Like the
rest, we were by nature objects of wrath.
⁴ But because of his great love for us, God,
who is rich in mercy, ⁵ made us alive with
Christ even when we were dead in
transgressions – it is by grace you have
been saved. ⁶ And God raised us up with
Christ and seated us with him in the
heavenly realms in Christ Jesus, ⁷ in order
that in the coming ages he might show the
incomparable riches of his grace, expressed
in his kindness to us in Christ Jesus. ⁸ For
it is by grace you have been saved, through
faith – and this not from yourselves, it is
the gift of God – ⁹ not by works, so that
no-one can boast. ¹⁰ For we are God's
workmanship, created in Christ Jesus to do
good works, which God prepared in
advance for us to do.

EXPLORE Paul spells out to the Christia
in Ephesus how our way of life deserv
God's anger (vs 1–3). We ignored Goc
commands and followed a way that
seemed full of life but was really
spiritually dead. But – and what a
glorious 'but' it is – God offers us the
gift of life because he loves us. This is
the 'grace' of God: totally undeserved
goodness shown to us by God, who
offers us the gift of life at the expense
of Christ's life. No one can earn this g
(vs 8,9) – we have only to accept it.

   No one can say, 'I've done a lot of
good things, so God will love me'; we
were all self-centred, and had decided
we knew how to run our lives better
than the one who had created us (v 3
We certainly didn't deserve being mac
alive and saved from death (v 5). Grac
has been defined as 'God's Riches At
Christ's Expense' (v 7), and those riche
which all stem from God's incomparab
love, are for us. This wonderful love
means that our lives are in the best
possible hands. No wonder Christians
write and sing songs of thanks!

RESPOND To help you express your thanks
to God, why not write a 'thank you' letter
long or short, to thank him for his gift to
you? You can then use what you've writte
as a prayer.

Day 5

Welcome to the family!

PREPARE When we become Christians, there's more to it than just joining a church, or belonging to a club, or choosing a particular set of beliefs that appeal to us. We are spiritually 're-born', into a huge family – the family of God. We take up our position in this family and are loved, needed and welcomed. How does this thought make you feel?

Philippians 1:1–11

Paul and Timothy, servants of Christ Jesus,

To all the saints in Christ Jesus at Philippi, together with the overseers and deacons:
² Grace and peace to you from God our Father and the Lord Jesus Christ.
³ I thank my God every time I remember you. ⁴ In all my prayers for all of you, I always pray with joy ⁵ because of your partnership in the gospel from the first day until now, ⁶ being confident of this, that he who began a good work in you will carry it on to completion until the day of Christ Jesus.
⁷ It is right for me to feel this way about all of you, since I have you in my heart; for whether I am in chains or defending and confirming the gospel, all of you share in God's grace with me. ⁸ God can testify how I long for all of you with the affection of Christ Jesus.
⁹ And this is my prayer: that your love may abound more and more in knowledge and depth of insight, ¹⁰ so that you may be able to discern what is best and may be pure and blameless until the day of Christ, ¹¹ filled with the fruit of righteousness that comes through Jesus Christ – to the glory and praise of God.

EXPLORE The church in Philippi, a large Roman town in northern Macedonia, had only been in existence for a few years, and the Christians were still young in their faith. But Paul, that great man of God, writes to them as equals (v 1), as partners in the work of proclaiming the gospel (v 5) – that is, the good news of Jesus – and as those who share God's grace with him (v 7); look at verse 12 too, where he calls them 'brothers'. Paul is not being patronising or falsely humble: what he is saying is true of the Philippians, and of us. The minute we become a committed follower of Jesus, then we are part of the family of God. God has no favourites, and our status in the world is of no account. What a wonderful thought! Each one of us is a special child of God, loved, cherished and cared for by the perfect Father.

But Paul knows too that babies in the faith need to grow to maturity. His prayer in verses 9–11 is for all of us. We need to grow in understanding and insight (v 9), be able to see evil clearly and avoid it, however deceptive the situation (v 10), and show in our lives the goodness that comes as we 'grow up' and gradually become like Jesus (v 11), secure in the love of God's family.

RESPOND Pray something like this: 'Thank you, Father, for bringing me, your loved and cherished child into your family.'

Day 6

SOS

Romans 5:1–11

Therefore, since we have been justified through faith, we have peace with God through our Lord Jesus Christ, [2] through whom we have gained access by faith into this grace in which we now stand. And we rejoice in the hope of the glory of God. [3] Not only so, but we also rejoice in our sufferings, because we know that suffering produces perseverance; [4] perseverance, character; and character, hope. [5] And hope does not disappoint us, because God has poured out his love into our hearts by the Holy Spirit, whom he has given us.

[6] You see, at just the right time, when we were still powerless, Christ died for the ungodly. [7] Very rarely will anyone die for a righteous man, though for a good man someone might possibly dare to die. [8] But God demonstrates his own love for us in this: While we were still sinners, Christ died for us.

[9] Since we have now been justified by his blood, how much more shall we be saved from God's wrath through him! [10] For if, when we were God's enemies, we were reconciled to him through the death of his Son, how much more, having been reconciled, shall we be saved through his life! [11] Not only is this so, but we also rejoice in God through our Lord Jesus Christ, through whom we have now received reconciliation.

EXPLORE Don't worry if you didn't follow everything in the passage; Paul's letter to Christians in Rome contains some of the deepest teaching in the Bible!

God created everything, including each one of us, yet we pushed him out of our lives. Because of this we deserve his anger and punishment (which involves eternal separation from everything that is good, beautiful and loving). But through Jesus we have been saved from that punishment (vs 1,8). From being enemies of God (v 10) we share with him in all that is good (v 2).

But 'being saved' does not guarantee prosperity and wealth. Anyone who says we only have to 'claim' health or wealth and it will be ours is teaching a cruel illusion. Paul knows that Christians will always face suffering and hardship, partly as a result of persecution for our faith and partly because we continue to live in a fallen world. But this suffering can be turned to our good, producing resilient and strong character (vs 3,4).

Ships in trouble used to send out SOS messages in Morse code – *Save our Souls*. Be assured that our souls have been saved – not by a lifeboat, but by the death and resurrection of Jesus (v 10).

RESPOND Reflect on this: We were God's enemies, but he made us his friends through the death of his Son.

Day 7

Destination – heaven!

PREPARE What do you think heaven is like? Thousands of Christians over the centuries have tried to describe it, but no one really knows. The reading today is from a vision that God gave to one of Jesus' disciples. Ask God to help you understand the promises he gives *you*.

Revelation 21:1–8

Then I saw a new heaven and a new earth, for the first heaven and the first earth had passed away, and there was no longer any sea. ² I saw the Holy City, the new Jerusalem, coming down out of heaven from God, prepared as a bride beautifully dressed for her husband. ³ And I heard a loud voice from the throne saying, "Now the dwelling of God is with men, and he will live with them. They will be his people, and God himself will be with them and be their God. ⁴ He will wipe every tear from their eyes. There will be no more death or mourning or crying or pain, for the old order of things has passed away."

⁵ He who was seated on the throne said, "I am making everything new!" Then he said, "Write this down, for these words are trustworthy and true."

⁶ He said to me: "It is done. I am the Alpha and the Omega, the Beginning and the End. To him who is thirsty I will give to drink without cost from the spring of the water of life. ⁷ He who overcomes will inherit all this, and I will be his God and he will be my son. ⁸ But the cowardly, the unbelieving, the vile, the murderers, the sexually immoral, those who practise magic arts, the idolaters and all liars – their place will be in the fiery lake of burning sulphur. This is the second death."

EXPLORE Revelation is full of imagery and allegory, and is therefore perhaps one of the more difficult books of the Bible to understand. However, Revelation is still God's word to us today, and we can read some exciting, comforting and very wonderful things about what lies in store for us after our death. Heaven is definitely going to be something totally new (v 5) that we have never experienced before. There will be a community of believers living close to God as his children (v 7). There will be no suffering or sorrow, no pain or tears (v 4). The old world as we know it – ruined by the sin of humans – will not exist (v 1); the place where we will live will be everything God intended and created our world to be.

Who will be there? Heaven is a place for believers in Jesus, for those who have responded to his invitation (v 6) and have not given up their faith in times of adversity (v 7). Those who reject his invitation face a different, dreadful destiny (v 8). There is no comfort here for those who think we will all get to heaven in the end, regardless of what we believe in. Accepting Jesus has always been the only way: there is nothing before or beyond him (v 6), nothing extra to do or believe. Jesus is all we need.

RESPOND Pray for those you know who have not yet accepted Jesus' invitation.

Day 8

How can I be sure?

PREPARE We are all different, and becoming a Christian affects us differently. Some people are like shaken-up fizzy drinks, others don't feel different at all. Perhaps you are like that, wondering how you can be sure you really are a child of God. Tell God how you feel.

Ephesians 1:3–14

3 Praise be to the God and Father of our Lord Jesus Christ, who has blessed us in the heavenly realms with every spiritual blessing in Christ. 4 For he chose us in him before the creation of the world to be holy and blameless in his sight. In love 5 he predestined us to be adopted as his sons through Jesus Christ, in accordance with his pleasure and will – 6 to the praise of his glorious grace, which he has freely given us in the One he loves. 7 In him we have redemption through his blood, the forgiveness of sins, in accordance with the riches of God's grace 8 that he lavished on us with all wisdom and understanding. 9 And he made known to us the mystery of his will according to his good pleasure, which he purposed in Christ, 10 to be put into effect when the times will have reached their fulfilment – to bring all things in heaven and on earth together under one head, even Christ.

11 In him we were also chosen, having been predestined according to the plan of him who works out everything in conformity with the purpose of his will, 12 in order that we, who were the first to hope in Christ, might be for the praise of his glory. 13 And you also were included in Christ when you heard the word of truth, the gospel of your salvation. Having believed, you were marked in him with a seal, the promised Holy Spirit, 14 who is a deposit guaranteeing our inheritance until the redemption of those who are God's possession – to the praise of his glory.

EXPLORE When we sign a contract, perhaps to buy a house, we have to pu down a deposit of money to indicate that we are serious. Once that deposit paid, no one else can have the goods. This is exactly what Paul is saying at th end of this passage: we belong to Go and no one can snatch us away, becau he has marked us with a deposit – his Holy Spirit in our hearts (vs 13,14; lool also at 2 Corinthians 1:21,22, which sa the same thing in a slightly different way). Before he gets to those crucial verses, he describes what we are as Christians: blessed, chosen and loved b God (vs 3–5), redeemed by the death Jesus (v 7; meaning 'bought back') an given insight, through Jesus, into God will for us (vs 9, 10). Paul uses the wor 'predestined' (vs 5,11), meaning 'dete mined beforehand'. But he doesn't mean that we play no part in becomin a Christian, because we all have free w to accept or reject God. He means tha we are part of God's overall plan for humanity, a plan that is not bound by time. However we feel – fizzy or quiet we became part of that plan when we heard the truth and said, 'That's for m (v 13). God guarantees it by his depos of the Holy Spirit within us.

RESPOND Some words of Jesus to think about: 'Whoever comes to me I will never drive away' (John 6:37). Perhaps you coulc learn these words – many Christians find i very helpful to memorise Bible verses.

14

Day 9

Trust and obey

PREPARE As Christians, there are things that Jesus asks us to do – things which can sometimes seem very hard. Over the next seven days we will read about some of these things. Ask God to show you how these readings apply to your own life.

When you were a child, did you always do as you were told? What difference did it make who was telling you? In medieval times, the common people owed allegiance to a lord. They had no choice: their birth into a family that belonged to the lord or chieftain ensured their loyalty. When we acknowledge Jesus as our Lord, we willingly and voluntarily put our lives under his control. This means that we will go along with his plans for our lives. We obey him – not out of fear of punishment, but because we love him, trust him and want to please him.

Genesis 12:1–9

The LORD had said to Abram, "Leave your country, your people and your father's household and go to the land I will show you.

2 "I will make you into a great nation
   and I will bless you;
will make your name great,
   and you will be a blessing.
I will bless those who bless you,
   and whoever curses you I will curse;
and all peoples on earth
   will be blessed through you."

So Abram left, as the LORD had told him; and Lot went with him. Abram was seventy-five years old when he set out from Haran. 5 He took his wife Sarai, his nephew Lot, all the possessions they had accumulated and the people they had acquired in Haran, and they set out for the land of Canaan, and they arrived there.

6 Abram travelled through the land as far as the site of the great tree of Moreh at Shechem. At that time the Canaanites were in the land. 7 The LORD appeared to Abram and said, "To your offspring I will give this land." So he built an altar there to the LORD, who had appeared to him.

8 From there he went on towards the hills east of Bethel and pitched his tent, with Bethel on the west and Ai on the east. There he built an altar to the LORD and called on the name of the LORD. 9 ...

EXPLORE (Note: Abram and Sarai are the same people as Abraham and Sarah. God changes their names in chapter 17.)

Abram didn't know Jesus, of course, but he did know and worship the one true God, despite the fact that where he lived, many false gods were worshipped. When he hears God's call to leave his settled and comfortable life, uproot his family and take them – plus livestock and servants – out into the unknown, he risks everything in order to obey.

In the same way, Jesus challenges us to venture everything in order to follow him (see Matthew 16:24–26). Obedience based on trust is vastly different from blind obedience, where we leave our brains behind! Our obedience to our Lord Jesus is trusting, intelligent obedience to a Lord who we know loves and cares for us more than we can ever imagine.

RESPOND Pray: 'Lord Jesus, I want to be obedient, because I love you. Please help me when I find it difficult.'

Day 10

Sin is serious

PREPARE Adam and Eve, have been given a beautiful, well-watered land to live in. But God has told them specifically that they must not eat the fruit of the tree of knowledge of good and evil, or they will die. We're about to find out what sin is.

Genesis 3

Now the serpent was more crafty than any of the wild animals the LORD God had made. He said to the woman, "Did God really say, 'You must not eat from any tree in the garden'?"

² The woman said to the serpent, " ... God did say, 'You must not eat fruit from the tree that is in the middle of the garden ... or you will die.'"

⁴ "You will not surely die," the serpent said ... ⁵ "For God knows that when you eat of it ... you will be like God, knowing good and evil." ⁶ When the woman saw that the fruit of the tree was good for food and pleasing to the eye, and also desirable for gaining wisdom, she took some and ate it. She also gave some to her husband, who was with her, and he ate it. ⁷ Then the eyes of both of them were opened, and they realised that they were naked; so they ... made coverings for themselves.

⁸ Then the man and his wife heard the sound of the LORD God as he was walking in the garden ... and they hid from the LORD God ... ⁹ But the LORD God called to the man, "Where are you?"

¹⁰ He answered, "I heard you in the garden, and I was afraid because I was naked; so I hid."

¹¹ And he said, "Who told you that you were naked? ..."

¹² The man said, "The woman you put here with me – she gave me some fruit from the tree, and I ate it."

¹³ Then the LORD God said to the woman, "What is this you have done?"
The woman said, "The serpent deceived me, and I ate." ...

EXPLORE Sin is disobedience to God. When Adam and Eve were disobedien their action had monumental consequ ences lasting to today. The relationshi between God and humans was broken and fear replaced fellowship (v 10). G cannot tolerate sin, because to do so would be a contradiction of what he i perfect and good – holy. Sin deserves punishment, and Adam and Eve were banished from the Garden of Eden an fellowship with God (vs 22,23). The consequences for humans and the wo have been immense. The physical wor is cursed, resulting in a hostile environment (vs 17,18). Relationships are distorted, and life brings pain and eventually death (vs 16,17,19).

Adam and Eve please themselves an seek equality with God (v 5). Humanit remains essentially self-centred, not God-centred (v 6), unwilling to see its actions as sinful and against God's law (vs 12,13). History shows our greed an desire for power and control at both national and individual levels. Because of this inherent sinfulness, we are unable to restore our relationship with God. Only when God sent his Son, Jes to bear the punishment for our sins could that broken relationship be restored, and the intimacy that God intended (vs 8,9) be re-established.

RESPOND Spend some time talking to Go and thanking him in prayer for the new relationship you have with him

16

Day 11

I'm *really* sorry...

PREPARE We are all sorry for things we have done, although our apologies to the injured person can be a bit half-hearted if we think they were 'just as much to blame' as we were! We can be filled with remorse, too, if we can see that our actions have caused real distress or injury. But this is not what the Bible calls repentance; repentance is more than sorrow or remorse, as we shall see today. Is there anything you are truly sorry about? Think about this as you read today's passage – one of the psalms of David.

Psalm 51

1 Have mercy on me, O God,
  according to your unfailing love;
  according to your great compassion
  blot out my transgressions.
2 Wash away all my iniquity
  and cleanse me from my sin. ...
4 Against you, you only, have I sinned
  and done what is evil in your sight, ...
5 Surely I was sinful at birth, ...
6 Surely you desire truth in the inner parts;
  you teach me wisdom ...
7 Cleanse me with hyssop, and I shall be
    clean; wash me, and I shall be whiter
    than snow.
8 Let me hear joy and gladness;
  let the bones you have crushed rejoice.
9 Hide your face from my sins
  and blot out all my iniquity.
10 Create in me a pure heart, O God,
  and renew a steadfast spirit within me.
11 Do not cast me from your presence
  or take your Holy Spirit from me.
12 Restore to me the joy of your salvation
  and grant me a willing spirit, to sustain
    me.
13 Then I will teach transgressors your
    ways,
  and sinners will turn back to you. ...
15 O Lord, open my lips,
  and my mouth will declare your praise.
16 You do not delight in sacrifice, or I
    would bring it; ...
17 The sacrifices of God are a broken spirit;
  a broken and contrite heart,
    O God, you will not despise. ...

EXPLORE The psalmist is not just sorry for what he has done, he has come to understand that his real sin is against God (v 4), in rebelling against him and his good purpose. When we choose our way instead of God's way, we are always wrong (v 4). Our selfish, sinful nature (v 5), which we inherited from Adam and Eve (as we saw yesterday), is known as our fallen nature. This fallen nature is always struggling for supremacy, and it is only by learning about God and his right ways that we can begin to change (v 6).

Do you notice how the psalmist doesn't make any excuses for his conduct? He doesn't say, 'I couldn't help it', or, 'It wasn't my fault'. Nor does he try to justify himself (in fact, we'll read about being justified tomorrow). He simply acknowledges that he has sinned and needs cleansing (v 2), needing the filth that is sin to be washed away by God (v 7). Real repentance involves taking the responsibility for our own sinful actions, acknowledging them to God and then turning right away from them. Then we can know, like the psalmist, that God forgives us.

RESPOND Why not use all or part of verses 1–4 as a prayer, confessing to God those things you have been thinking about for which you are sorry?

Day 12

I'm forgiven!

PREPARE In our heart of hearts we all know that what we do wrong has to be paid for. We talk about 'getting away with it', implying that we know full well we could have been caugh and 'made to pay'. Some people refuse to listen to their conscience, blotting out its voice u it hardly exists. Many others carry a burden of guilt for past offences or actions which cripp them emotionally for years after, feeling that they can never forgive themselves. But the go news is that this need not be. Think back to the things you confessed yesterday as you read another part of Paul's letter to Christians in Rome (don't worry if you don't follow it all).

Romans 3:21–26

21 But now a righteousness from God, apart from law, has been made known, to which the Law and the Prophets testify. 22 This righteousness from God comes through faith in Jesus Christ to all who believe. There is no difference, 23 for all have sinned and fall short of the glory of God, 24 and are justified freely by his grace through the redemption that came by Christ Jesus. 25 God presented him as a sacrifice of atonement, through faith in his blood. He did this to demonstrate his justice, because in his forbearance he had left the sins committed beforehand unpunished 26 – he did it to demonstrate his justice at the present time, so as to be just and the one who justifies those who have faith in Jesus.

EXPLORE God has totally forgiven us, and our sin does not appear in his heavenly 'account book'. God has not done this because our sins weren't ver serious, or because we had tried hard be good, or because our good deeds cancelled out our bad deeds. He has forgiven us, and restored our relationship with him, because Jesus, h Son, died on the cross for us ('a sacrifi of atonement', v 25): God himself too the punishment on our behalf. The NIV uses the word 'justified' in verse 24 to describe this restored relationship; it means 'declared righteous' – declared morally right in God's eyes. Think of it as meaning '*just as if I'd never sinned*'.

This restored relationship is a free g from God, but we have to accept it, taking it in our hands and saying, 'Thank you; I know I don't deserve it.' We have to own up to our sin, and believe in Jesus (v 26) as the living revelation of God, who forgives.

RESPOND A verse to think about: 'I, even am he who blots out your transgressions, for my own sake, and remembers your sin no more' (Isaiah 43:25).

Day 13

Forgiving others

PREPARE **Start today with this prayer from Psalm 86:11: 'Teach me your way, O Lord, and I will walk in your truth'. When we talk about forgiving others, we need to sort out our way of thinking, and discover what Jesus meant. Christian forgiveness is not condoning the sin, or simply forgetting all about it: we are forgiving the person who has injured us, not trying to excuse or diminish their action. And Christian forgiveness is not conditional: we are not saying we will only forgive if the act is not repeated, or if the person is truly sorry. So what is it?**

Matthew 18:21–35

21 Then Peter came to Jesus and asked, "Lord, how many times shall I forgive my brother when he sins against me? ..."
22 Jesus answered, "I tell you, not seven times, but seventy-seven times.
23 "Therefore, the kingdom of heaven is like a king who wanted to settle accounts ... 24 As he began ... a man who owed him ten thousand talents was brought to him.
25 Since he was not able to pay, the master ordered that he and his wife and his children and all that he had be sold to repay the debt.
26 "The servant fell on his knees before him. 'Be patient with me,' he begged ...
27 The servant's master took pity on him, cancelled the debt and let him go.
28 "But when that servant went out, he found one of his fellow-servants who owed him a hundred denarii. He grabbed him and began to choke him. 'Pay back what you owe me!' he demanded.
... he went off and had the man thrown into prison until he could pay the debt.
31 When the other servants saw what had happened, they ... went and told their master everything that had happened.
32 "Then the master called the servant in. 'You wicked servant,' he said, 'I cancelled all that debt of yours because you begged me to. 33 Shouldn't you have had mercy on your fellow-servant just as I had on you?' 34 In anger his master turned him over ... to be tortured, until he should pay back all he owed. ..."

EXPLORE **The servant could not possibly repay the money he owed to the king – and the king wiped it right out of the account book. We saw yesterday that this is what God does when we repent: he deletes our sin, and treats us as if we had never sinned. We are called to forgive in the same way. Do you sometimes feel you could never forgive someone? Our feelings are not reliable guides to what we should do: Jesus tells us that we are to forgive as God has forgiven us (Matthew 6:12). The unforgiving servant in the parable acted as so many of us do: although his own debt was cancelled, he harboured grievances and grudges and tried to make others pay.**

It is never easy to forgive someone who has done us a great wrong or injury. Jesus knew that bitterness and longing for revenge would sour our hearts and injure our inner lives; but however much we would like it to be otherwise, his teaching on forgiveness is crystal clear. God's way is for us to forgive others, just as he has forgiven us, because a truly repentant heart is a forgiving heart.

RESPOND **Are you holding any grudges against anyone, even from a long time ago, that need putting right? Putting right may involve both forgiveness and action.**

Day 14

New priorities

PREPARE When we put on clothes, we present an image to the world. Depending on circumstances, or how we feel, we may want to look businesslike or casual and easygoing, t‹ stand out or be discreet. What sort of image do you want to show to the world? Has this changed since you became a Christian?

Colossians 3:1–14

Since, then, you have been raised with Christ, set your hearts on things above, where Christ is seated at the right hand of God. ² Set your minds on things above, not on earthly things. ³ For you died, and your life is now hidden with Christ in God. ⁴ When Christ, who is your life, appears, then you also will appear with him in glory.

⁵ Put to death, therefore, whatever belongs to your earthly nature: sexual immorality, impurity, lust, evil desires and greed, which is idolatry. ⁶ Because of these, the wrath of God is coming. ⁷ You used to walk in these ways, in the life you once lived. ⁸ But now you must rid yourselves of all such things as these: anger, rage, malice, slander and filthy language from your lips. ⁹ Do not lie to each other, since you have taken off your old self with its practices ¹⁰ and have put on the new self, which is being renewed in knowledge in the image of its Creator. ¹¹ Here there is no Greek or Jew, circumcised or uncircumcised, barbarian, Scythian, slave or free, but Christ is all, and is in all.

¹² Therefore, as God's chosen people, holy and dearly loved, clothe yourselves with compassion, kindness, humility, gentleness and patience. ¹³ Bear with each other and forgive whatever grievances you may have against one another. Forgive as the Lord forgave you. ¹⁴ And over all these virtues put on love, which binds them all together in perfect unity.

EXPLORE (Notice how verse 13 bears o‹ what we learnt yesterday about forgive ness. 'Cross-referencing' is an importan‹ part of Bible reading, building up our understanding by seeing what differen‹ parts of the Bible say about something.

As Christians, our priorities will begi‹ to change. What seemed so important status, our own interests – are now of no account (vs 1–3). But Paul (who wrote this letter to the Christians at Colossae) knows full well the greed, selfishness and immorality that lies at the heart of all people (v 7). Now, though, he says we are to put other things first – no longer our own desire wishes and passions (vs 5,8,9). When ‹ are Christians we 'get dressed' in a different way (vs 9,10,12). From being selfish and greedy, we are to 'put on' compassion, kindness, humility, gentleness and patience (v 12). We ha‹ to make a real effort to put on these beautiful Christian qualities. But we do it because we choose to love each oth‹ (v 14), not simply because we are told to! And we are given the ability to do this because we are God's chosen people, and because he loves us. We a‹ to be very different from the world today, torn apart by racial tensions, terrorism, hatred and greed.

RESPOND Pray: 'Thank you, Lord, that you love me dearly as your child. Help me to show this love to others in the way I behav‹

Day 15

Making time for God

PREPARE How difficult do you find it to sit down quietly, alone with God? Does it seem like an unjustified luxury when there is so much else to do? Ask God to help you feel free from pressure as you take time to be with him.

Luke 10:38–42

38 As Jesus and his disciples were on their way, he came to a village where a woman named Martha opened her home to him. 39 She had a sister called Mary, who sat at the Lord's feet listening to what he said. 40 But Martha was distracted by all the preparations that had to be made. She came to him and asked, "Lord, don't you care that my sister has left me to do the work by myself? Tell her to help me!"
41 "Martha, Martha," the Lord answered, "you are worried and upset about many things, 42 but only one thing is needed. Mary has chosen what is better, and it will not be taken away from her."

EXPLORE Martha was doing her best to welcome Jesus, bustling around putting on an elaborate meal for the crowd. Women had a subordinate role in Jewish society, and were expected to be at the beck and call of the men. Listening to Jesus was not Mary's place as a dutiful hostess! Perhaps Martha is doubly angry with Mary, who not only leaves her to do all the work that she considers necessary but who also does not keep to 'her place' in the background. Surely Jesus will see how wrong this all is?

But Jesus' reply gives Martha – and us – a lot to think about. Martha's busyness is self-imposed and not necessary. Mary has chosen the right thing in seizing the chance to learn from Jesus, despite society's expectations. We too – both men and women – need to give time to listen to and learn from God. The most natural time for this is as we read the Bible and pray. Both activities need periods of listening. God cannot speak to us if we keep talking to him all the time! To do this, busy lives may need rescheduling, and some activities may need to go in order to give God room to speak and act in our lives. God is not an optional extra. He is Lord.

RESPOND Consider your daily and weekly routines. Is there anything you think God might want you to change? As you read your Bible, give yourself time to mull it over. Does anything strike you particularly or seem especially relevant to your life?

Day 16

To God be the glory!

PREPARE When we fall in love with someone, we want to get to know them better, spend time with them, talk with them, find out how to please them. Getting to know God is an important part of our Christian life. Over the next eight days we will look at ways in which we can build our relationship with God.

'Worship' is not just singing hymns or songs, or going to church, though it does include these things. True worship is our own response to God, an expression of our own relationship with him. What have you learnt about God that makes you glad? Tell him now!

Romans 11:33 – 12:2

11:33 Oh, the depth of the riches of the wisdom and knowledge of God!
How unsearchable his judgements, and his paths beyond tracing out!
34 "Who has known the mind of the Lord? Or who has been his counsellor?"
35 "Who has ever given to God, that God should repay him?"
36 For from him and through him and to him are all things.
To him be the glory for ever! Amen.
12:1 Therefore, I urge you, brothers, in view of God's mercy, to offer your bodies as living sacrifices, holy and pleasing to God – this is your spiritual act of worship. 2 Do not conform any longer to the pattern of this world, but be transformed by the renewing of your mind. Then you will be able to test and approve what God's will is – his good, pleasing and perfect will.

EXPLORE Paul bursts into a hymn of praise, giving many reasons why we should worship God. God's rich and immense wisdom and knowledge surpass anything we can aspire to (11:33); we cannot possibly criticise him or think we know better (11:34). Everything comes from God, is upheld by him and points towards him (11:36). In view of all this, the only response we can possibly make is to regard the whole of our life (our 'bodies') as an act of worship (12:1). We bring glory to God by what we do and the way we live, not only on Sundays but every day. We cannot honour God properly if we still cling to our old standards or allow society to impose its practices on us. Our minds must be made new; we need to think as those who belong completely to God, so that what he wants is what we want (12:2).

The expression of our worship can take many forms: for example, a torrent of adoring words, a deep meditative silence, a creative gift or an act of loving service which may be costly to us. No one way is better than another. If it is a real expression of our love, it is acceptable to God.

RESPOND Think: How will you express your worship of God during this week?

Day 17

Hallelujah! Praise the Lord!

PREPARE Start today by praising God with these words from Psalm 118:28: 'You are my God, and I will give thanks; you are my God, and I will exalt you.'
From the very earliest days of the church, the believers gathered together to sing their praises and give thanks (see Acts 2:42–47), and used the Psalms in doing so. Christians everywhere still use the Psalms in this way today, and many of our greatest hymns and modern worship songs are based on the Psalms.

Psalm 150

¹ Praise the LORD.

Praise God in his sanctuary;
  praise him in his mighty heavens.
² Praise him for his acts of power;
  praise him for his surpassing greatness.
³ Praise him with the sounding of the
    trumpet,
  praise him with the harp and lyre,
⁴ praise him with tambourine and dancing,
  praise him with the strings and flute,
⁵ praise him with the clash of cymbals,
  praise him with resounding cymbals.
⁶ Let everything that has breath praise the
  LORD.

Praise the LORD.

EXPLORE Like the psalmist, we praise God for who he is (v 1) and for what he does (v 2). Praise and thanksgiving go with music and song like love goes with hugs (vs 3–6) – what's inside is being expressed. It is hard to exclaim 'Hallelujah!' (a Hebrew word meaning 'Praise the Lord', used in verses 1 and 6 of this psalm) more than twice without a lilt coming into our voices. We may want to express our celebrations and praises by lifting our hands, or with dancing and clapping. Congregations everywhere enjoy singing hymns or songs where they can really let rip and raise the roof And why not? Our God is a great and wonderful God: let's praise him with all our hearts, minds and voices!

Many of our greatest and loveliest hymns and songs express both our praises and our thanks. But although we can sing out our praises, alone or in the company of others, we often want to express our thanks in a more tangible way. Just as we will send some flowers or a gift as a 'thank you' for a special act of hospitality or service, so we want to give to God to express our thanks for all he has done (we will come back to this on Day 23).

RESPOND You might like to try writing your own short psalm or praise song. Or perhaps simply explore the Psalms and make some of them your own songs to God.

Day 18

What is prayer?

PREPARE **Why do you think people pray?**

Nehemiah 1

... ³ "Those who survived the exile and are back in the province are in great trouble and disgrace. The wall of Jerusalem is broken down, and its gates have been burned with fire."

⁴ When I heard these things, I sat down and wept. For some days I mourned and fasted and prayed before the God of heaven. ⁵ Then I said:

"O LORD, God of heaven, the great and awesome God, who keeps his covenant of love with those who love him and obey his commands, ⁶ let your ear be attentive and your eyes open to hear the prayer your servant is praying before you day and night for your servants, the people of Israel. I confess the sins we Israelites, including myself and my father's house, have committed against you. ⁷ We have acted very wickedly towards you. We have not obeyed the commands ... and laws ...

⁸ "Remember the instruction you gave your servant Moses, saying, 'If you are unfaithful, I will scatter you among the nations, ⁹ but if you return to me and obey my commands, then even if your exiled people are at the farthest horizon, I will gather them from there and bring them to the place I have chosen as a dwelling for my Name.'

¹⁰ "They are your servants and your people, whom you redeemed by your great strength and your mighty hand. ¹¹ O Lord, let your ear be attentive to the prayer of this your servant and to the prayer of your servants who delight in revering your name. Give your servant success today by granting him favour in the presence of this man." ...

EXPLORE We cannot have a relationship with someone unless we communicate with them. Prayer is the expression of our relationship with God. Prayer work in some way it releases God's supernatural power into a situation.

Nehemiah lived in Babylonia after the Jews had been exiled there and Jerusalem, their capital, had been destroyed 586 BC. Some exiles had returned, but Nehemiah is devastated when he learn that things have actually got worse in Jerusalem. He immediately turns to Go Who do we turn to in moments of despair?

Prayers are not just 'shopping lists'. Nehemiah first of all gives praise and thanksgiving for the greatness and faithfulness of God (v 5); he goes on repent of his own and his people's sin (vs 6,7); and only then does he ask for God's help. But prayer is not asking G to do what we want! Nehemiah know that God is calling him to act in this difficult situation, but he also knows that he must leave the timing and arrangements in God's hands. It was four months before God created an opportunity for him to approach the king. How long are we prepared to wa for answers to prayer? God wants us t be like Nehemiah: to keep praying, to keep asking and to wait patiently.

RESPOND Consider starting a prayer notebook or journal, keeping a record of your prayer requests and note the answer as you see them. Many Christians find doi this helpful and sometimes surprising!

Day 19

How do I pray?

PREPARE As a new Christian, it is sometimes the practicalities of prayer that prevent us getting going. Must I kneel? What do I say? What do I pray for?

Matthew 6:5–15

"And when you pray, do not be like the hypocrites, for they love to pray standing in the synagogues and on the street corners to be seen by men. I tell you the truth, they have received their reward in full. 6 But when you pray, go into your room, close the door and pray to your Father, who is unseen. Then your Father, who sees what is done in secret, will reward you. 7 And when you pray, do not keep on babbling like pagans, for they think they will be heard because of their many words. 8 Do not be like them, for your Father knows what you need before you ask him.

9 "This, then, is how you should pray:

" 'Our Father in heaven,
hallowed be your name,
10 your kingdom come,
your will be done
    on earth as it is in heaven.
11 Give us today our daily bread.
12 Forgive us our debts,
    as we also have forgiven our debtors.
13 And lead us not into temptation,
but deliver us from the evil one.'

14 For if you forgive men when they sin against you, your heavenly Father will also forgive you. 15 But if you do not forgive men their sins, your Father will not forgive your sins."

EXPLORE Firstly, says Jesus, prayer is between God the Father and you (v 6). In order to make sure that God is your focus, and not others (v 5), you might find it best to go somewhere on your own. Sometimes the only way we can be alone with God is to go for a walk, or take a bath, and that's fine! It doesn't matter whether you lie, sit, stand, kneel or move around: this is your time with God, whatever length, and you need to do what you feel most comfortable with. Some will find it easiest to schedule a regular time for prayer and Bible reading, whilst others delight in the unexpected and prefer to take unplanned opportunities. What is important is to be sincere. The number of words is not important: it is what we say, not how long our prayers are, that matters (v 7). And note that Jesus is not saying that we can only pray when we're alone: we can still pray silently wherever we are, whatever we are doing and whoever we are with. But we mustn't show off, like the Pharisees did (v 5).

Jesus gives us all the ingredients for a vibrant prayer life, a directory for our own prayers (vs 9–13).

RESPOND Make verses 9–13 your prayer today; pause after every line, and think how you could enlarge on that particular concept.

Day 20

Difficulties in prayer

PREPARE Does it worry you that you sometimes feel you can't pray? We all have moments **|**
that: we can't concentrate, God seems a million miles away and our prayers never get off th
ground! What's gone wrong?

Psalm 13

¹ How long, O Lord? Will you forget me
   for ever?
   How long will you hide your face from
   me?
² How long must I wrestle with my
   thoughts
   and every day have sorrow in my heart?
   How long will my enemy triumph over
   me?
³ Look on me and answer, O Lord my God.
   Give light to my eyes, or I will sleep in
   death;
⁴ my enemy will say, "I have overcome
   him,"
   and my foes will rejoice when I fall.
⁵ But I trust in your unfailing love;
   my heart rejoices in your salvation.
⁶ I will sing to the Lord,
   for he has been good to me.

EXPLORE The psalmist feels God has
forgotten him (v 1), he has lost all joy
life (vs 2,3) and everything is going
wrong (v 4). When we feel like that,
psalms like this can help. The psalmist
knows three things: God loves him (v
God is his salvation (v 5) and God has
been good to him in the past (v 6). So
regardless of how he feels (feelings ar
not always reliable), he holds on to
what he knows and trusts God to act.

When we struggle to pray, a frame-
work can give us the start we need. O
example is ACTS. **A**doration: tell God
you love him and want to praise him –
use the words of a hymn or song to
help here. **C**onfession: own up to wha
you have done wrong in God's eyes, a
ask his forgiveness. **T**hanksgiving: thar
God for all he has done, and that you
are his beloved child. **S**upplication: all
our requests, things we are asking eith
for ourselves or for others.

We usually think of prayer as speaki◼
to God in our own words, but there is
also a place for using formal or writter
prayers if helpful. As you read the Bibl
you will come across passages that yo▌
can use as prayers, particularly in the
psalms. You might like to write them
down, or memorise them, and use the▌
when you need their help. God will
always listen to prayers from your hea▌

† Augustine [AD 354–430], from *The Lion
Prayer Collection*, Mary Batchelor [ed],
1992.

RESPOND 'Father, I am seeking; I am hesita▮
and uncertain, but will you, O God, watch
over each step of mine and guide me' †

Day 21

Why read the Bible?

PREPARE What have you learnt from the Bible so far? It is possible to read the Bible without it meaning very much in a personal sense. As history, biography, poetry or literature, it can be interesting but it can also seem boring and irrelevant. After all, it all happened so long ago!

Luke 24:13–32

13 Now that same day two of them were going to a village called Emmaus ... 14 They were talking with each other about everything that had happened. 15 As they talked and discussed these things with each other, Jesus himself came up and walked along with them; 16 but they were kept from recognising him.
17 He asked them, "What are you discussing together ... ?" They stood still, their faces downcast. 18 One of them, named Cleopas, asked him, "Are you only a visitor to Jerusalem and do not know the things that have happened there ... ?"
19 "What things?" he asked.
"About Jesus of Nazareth," they replied. "He was a prophet, powerful in word and deed ... 20 The chief priests and our rulers ... crucified him; 21 but we had hoped that he was ... going to redeem Israel. ..."
25 He said to them, "How foolish you are, and how slow of heart to believe all that the prophets have spoken! ..." 27 And ... he explained to them what was said in all the Scriptures concerning himself.
28 As they approached the village ... Jesus acted as if he were going further. 29 But they urged him strongly, "Stay with us ..." So he went in to stay with them.
30 When he was at the table with them, he took bread, gave thanks, broke it and began to give it to them. 31 Then their eyes were opened and they recognised him, and he disappeared from their sight. 32 They asked each other, "Were not our hearts burning within us while he talked with us on the road and opened the Scriptures to us?"

EXPLORE The two disciples on the road to Emmaus, being good Jews, knew their Scriptures – what we now call the Old Testament. They would have been familiar with the history of great kings like David, and known about the promised Messiah – the Christ – who would redeem Israel (v 21). They were expecting the Messiah to be a military figure who would liberate them from the Romans. But they hadn't properly understood the Scriptures. When Jesus meets them, he explains to them clearly what the Scriptures really said about the Messiah – about himself (vs 25–27)! After his final, familiar gesture of breaking bread, the two disciples see: *now* their eyes are opened, *now* they understand, *now* their hearts have had the veils of ignorance burnt away (vs 30–32), and they understand what God has been saying all along.

We cannot say we know someone if we have only met them once. Relationships take time. We will meet Jesus, and understand more and more of him as we read God's Word. The Bible is not just history, it is his story. It is not just about Jesus: it is where we can meet Jesus. Everything that Jesus gave to his disciples he gives to us in the Bible: teaching, love, comfort, admonition, care. We need the Bible.

RESPOND Ask God to open your mind so that you can understand the Scriptures, just as Jesus did for the disciples in verse 45.

Day 22

A public proclamation

PREPARE **In the very early days of Christianity, when Peter, Paul and all the other disciples were confidently proclaiming the good news of the gospel, baptism followed belief as nigh follows day.**

Acts 2:22–41

22 "Men of Israel, listen to this: Jesus of Nazareth was a man accredited by God to you ... 23 This man was handed over to you by God's set purpose ... and you ... put him to death by nailing him to the cross. 24 But God raised him from the dead, freeing him from the agony of death, because it was impossible for death to keep its hold on him. 25 David said about him:

" 'I saw the Lord always before me.
Because he is at my right hand,
I will not be shaken. ...' "

29 "Brothers, ... he spoke of the resurrection of the Christ, that he was not abandoned to the grave, nor did his body see decay. 32 God has raised this Jesus to life, and we are all witnesses of the fact. 33 Exalted to the right hand of God, he has received from the Father the promised Holy Spirit and has poured out what you now see and hear. ..."
36 "Therefore let all Israel be assured of this: God has made this Jesus, whom you crucified, both Lord and Christ."
37 When the people heard this, they were cut to the heart and said to Peter and the other apostles, "Brothers, what shall we do?"
38 Peter replied, "Repent and be baptised, every one of you, in the name of Jesus Christ for the forgiveness of your sins. And you will receive the gift of the Holy Spirit. 39 The promise is for you and your children and for all who are far off – for all whom the Lord our God will call." ...
41 Those who accepted his message were baptised, and about three thousand were added to their number that day.

EXPLORE 'What shall we do?' asked the crowds, as Peter confronted them with the truth about Jesus (vs 32–36). Peter answer was short and clear (v 38). A mere verbal acquiescence to the messa was not enough. Having declared thei belief in Jesus, and a determination to turn away from sin, baptism was the next step for the believer and perhaps his or her family. It wasn't that baptisr *made* them into Christians. It was a symbolic act of dying to their old life a they were covered in water, and an important public proclamation of their faith and their new life. In later years, this was a courageous act, as Christian were to be harassed, persecuted and killed for their proclaimed faith.

Today, churches vary in their practic of baptism of adults or infants. In mar churches, parents bring their children be baptised into the church. The pare make their own commitment to bring the children up in the Christian faith. When the children become old enoug they confirm their own personal commitment to Jesus in a service of confirmation or church membership. Whatever form our public declaration takes – adult baptism by immersion, confirmation or any other ceremony – does not make us into Christians. We make this public act of commitment *because* we are Christians.

RESPOND **Think: Can I make a public act commitment to Jesus?**

Day 23

Giving to God

2 Corinthians 8:1–15

And now, brothers, we want you to know about the grace that God has given the Macedonian churches. 2 Out of the most severe trial, their overflowing joy and their extreme poverty welled up in rich generosity. 3 ... they gave as much as they were able, and even beyond their ability. Entirely on their own, 4 they urgently pleaded with us for the privilege of sharing in this service to the saints. 5 And they did not do as we expected, but they gave themselves first to the Lord and then to us in keeping with God's will. ... 7 But just as you excel in everything – in faith, in speech, in knowledge, in complete earnestness and in your love for us – see that you also excel in this grace of giving. 8 I ... want to test the sincerity of your love ... 9 For you know the grace of our Lord Jesus Christ, that though he was rich, yet for your sakes he became poor, so that you through his poverty might become rich. 10 And here is my advice about what is best for you in this matter: Last year you were the first not only to give but also to have the desire to do so. 11 Now finish the work, so that your eager willingness to do it may be matched by your completion of it, according to your means. 12 For if the willingness is there, the gift is acceptable according to what one has, not according to what he does not have. 13 Our desire is not that others might be relieved while you are hard pressed, but that there might be equality. ... 15 as it is written: "He who gathered much did not have too much, and he who gathered little did not have too little."

EXPLORE A relief fund has been set up by churches in Asia Minor and Macedonia to help poor Christians in Jerusalem (see 1 Corinthians 16:1–3). Paul urges the Corinthian church to give as generously as the Macedonians (vs 1– 4). Generosity is just as important as the other spiritual gifts God gives to Christians (v 7; look also at 1 Corinthians 1:4–7). Our example must always be Jesus, who gave up unknowable riches and glory (v 9). But Paul isn't just shouting 'Give! Give! Give!' He knows not everyone has a great deal to give, and assures them – and us – that 'If you are eager to give, God will accept your gift on the basis of what you have to give, not on what you haven't' (v 12, Good News Bible). Under the rules of the Old Testament law, Jews had to give a proportion of their income – a tithe – to God, in goods or money. In Jesus Christ, we are not bound by such rules, but the principle remains. First, we give to God what is right in our circumstances. Then we balance our budget.

We usually think of giving to God as a financial commitment, but there are other ways to give. Some can give their time and skills to be used in God's service, even if money is woefully short. There is always a place for a willing volunteer! How much can we give, not how little can we get away with?

Day 24

Becoming like Jesus

PREPARE 'I am the vine; you are the branches. If a man remains in me and I in him, he will bear much fruit; apart from me you can do nothing' (John 15:5).
   Over the next six days we will look at how God helps us to be the sort of people he wants us to be. How do you think you've changed since you became a Christian? Have you found some of it hard going?

1 Peter 1:13 – 2:3

1:13 Therefore, prepare your minds for action; be self-controlled; set your hope fully on the grace to be given you when Jesus Christ is revealed. 14 As obedient children, do not conform to the evil desires you had when you lived in ignorance. 15 But just as he who called you is holy, so be holy in all you do; 16 for it is written: "Be holy, because I am holy."

17 Since you call on a Father who judges each man's work impartially, live your lives as strangers here in reverent fear. 18 For you know that it was not with perishable things such as silver or gold that you were redeemed from the empty way of life handed down to you from your forefathers, 19 but with the precious blood of Christ, a lamb without blemish or defect. 20 He was chosen before the creation of the world, but was revealed in these last times for your sake. 21 Through him you believe in God, who raised him from the dead and glorified him, and so your faith and hope are in God.

22 Now that you have purified yourselves by obeying the truth so that you have sincere love for your brothers, love one another deeply, from the heart ...

2:1 Therefore, rid yourselves of all malice and all deceit, hypocrisy, envy, and slander of every kind. 2 Like newborn babies, crave pure spiritual milk, so that by it you may grow up in your salvation, 3 now that you have tasted that the Lord is good.

EXPLORE Peter is writing a general letter to Christians in the young churches in Asia Minor. They were no doubt discovering, as all Christians would throughout the ages, that living a holy life is far from easy! To be holy means to live a life of total moral perfection, as Jesus did. God is holy – he is perfect in everything – and he wants us to be like that! The process of becoming holy is known as sanctification, and it starts with love: our love for God and the love we truly have for our fellow humans (1:22). We must put aside 'evil desires' (1:14), thoughts that originate in our minds, such as the desires to do harm in any way, to want what others have, to pretend to be what we are not, to deceive others and to gossip (2:1). It is not enough that we do not act on these thoughts: we must put such ideas right out of our heads.

   God knows that becoming more holy is a continuing struggle for us, and we will never be completely holy until we get to heaven. But God has not left us to face this struggle on our own – we would have no hope in that case! God the Father has sent us his Holy Spirit, who is the means by which we can achieve the impossible and become more holy, more like Jesus, God's Son.

RESPOND The God who raised Jesus from the dead is more than able to make us ho

Day 25

Training for perfection

PREPARE As we saw yesterday, God tells us this: 'Be holy, because I am holy'. Today we meet the Holy Spirit, without whom it would be impossible. (Old translations of the Bible speak of him as the Holy Ghost, which may make him seem, unfairly, a bit spooky!)

John 14:15–27

15 "If you love me, you will obey what I command. 16 And I will ask the Father, and he will give you another Counsellor to be with you for ever – 17 the Spirit of truth. The world cannot accept him, because it neither sees him nor knows him. But you know him, for he lives with you and will be in you. 18 I will not leave you as orphans; I will come to you. 19 Before long, the world will not see me any more, but you will see me. Because I live, you also will live. 20 On that day you will realise that I am in my Father, and you are in me, and I am in you. 21 Whoever has my commands and obeys them, he is the one who loves me. He who loves me will be loved by my Father, and I too will love him and show myself to him."

22 Then Judas (not Judas Iscariot) said, 'But, Lord, why do you intend to show yourself to us and not to the world?"

23 Jesus replied, "If anyone loves me, he will obey my teaching. My Father will love him, and we will come to him and make our home with him. 24 He who does not love me will not obey my teaching. These words you hear are not my own; they belong to the Father who sent me.

25 "All this I have spoken while still with you. 26 But the Counsellor, the Holy Spirit, whom the Father will send in my name, will teach you all things and will remind you of everything I have said to you. 27 Peace I leave with you; my peace I give you. I do not give to you as the world gives. Do not let your hearts be troubled and do not be afraid.2

EXPLORE Sports stars always get a lot of publicity. But behind successful sportspeople are their coaches. The New Testament was originally written in Greek, and the Greek name for the Holy Spirit is *parakletos*; this means something like 'one who comes alongside' to help, encourage, train, point out what is wrong, comfort and counsel. The Holy Spirit is like our own individual sports coach, but much more!

Jesus promised he would not leave his disciples as orphans (v 18). For three years he had been with them, 'coaching' them in this radically new way of life. On the eve of his death he promises to send the Counsellor, the Spirit of truth (vs 16,17) who will be with them – and with every believer – for all time.

This is the Holy Spirit, who comes to live in us and be alongside us (v 17) when we commit our lives to Jesus. We see the wholeness of the Trinity (Father, Son and Holy Spirit): Jesus says that both he and God the Father will live in us when we love and believe in Jesus (v 23) because the Holy Spirit will live in us. The Spirit's work is to counsel and encourage us, remind us of Jesus' teaching and, ultimately, make us like Jesus. When that happens, it will be far more wonderful than any number of Olympic gold medals!

RESPOND Prayer: Thank you Jesus, that you never leave us on our own, but that your Spirit is here to help and encourage us.

Day 26

Filled to the brim

Acts 1:1–8

In my former book, Theophilus, I wrote about all that Jesus began to do and to teach ^{2} until the day he was taken up to heaven, after giving instructions through the Holy Spirit to the apostles he had chosen. ^{3} After his suffering, he showed himself to these men and gave many convincing proofs that he was alive. He appeared to them over a period of forty days and spoke about the kingdom of God. ^{4} On one occasion, while he was eating with them, he gave them this command: "Do not leave Jerusalem, but wait for the gift my Father promised, which you have heard me speak about. ^{5} For John baptised with water, but in a few days you will be baptised with the Holy Spirit."

^{6} So when they met together, they asked him, "Lord, are you at this time going to restore the kingdom to Israel?"

^{7} He said to them: "It is not for you to know the times or dates the Father has set by his own authority. ^{8} But you will receive power when the Holy Spirit comes on you; and you will be my witnesses in Jerusalem, and in all Judea and Samaria, and to the ends of the earth."

EXPLORE As we read yesterday, when we become Christians, the Holy Spirit comes into our lives. Here Jesus speaks of the Holy Spirit's coming as a baptism, when power would come upon the disciples as they spread the news of Jesus through the world (vs 5,8). A lot has been written about 'baptism in the Holy Spirit'. The original Greek word for baptism means something like a thorough soaking, and whilst for some Christians that 'soaking' has undoubtedly been dynamic, like a sprinter bursting out of his blocks, for others it has been slowly building up over time, more like a long-distance runner!

However, whichever way we are initially drenched by the Spirit, it is absolutely certain that we all need constant refilling. We can see this by looking at Ephesians 5:18, where Paul tells us to 'be filled with the Spirit'. The idea is of a *continuous* process: not 'be filled once', but '*go on* being filled'. As containers we are woefully unsatisfactory: our humanity and inherent sinfulness make us very leaky! We continually need to repent of our sinfulness and ask God to fill us with the Holy Spirit – and he will answer (see Luke 11:13)! It is through the Spirit that we receive the power that is promised to help us live for and serve God (v 8)

Day 27

Getting better

PREPARE 'Be holy, because I am holy.' The idea of the Holy Spirit working in power in us may make us feel a bit nervous: will he make us do things we don't want to do? Or perhaps we think we might become a sort of spiritual Superman or Superwoman! But it isn't like that – although God *can* surprise and delight us! The work of the Holy Spirit is to make us like Jesus.

Galatians 5:16–26

16 So I say, live by the Spirit, and you will not gratify the desires of the sinful nature. 17 For the sinful nature desires what is contrary to the Spirit, and the Spirit what is contrary to the sinful nature. They are in conflict with each other, so that you do not do what you want. 18 But if you are led by the Spirit, you are not under law.

19 The acts of the sinful nature are obvious: sexual immorality, impurity and debauchery; 20 idolatry and witchcraft; hatred, discord, jealousy, fits of rage, selfish ambition, dissensions, factions 21 and envy; drunkenness, orgies, and the like. I warn you, as I did before, that those who live like this will not inherit the kingdom of God.

22 But the fruit of the Spirit is love, joy, peace, patience, kindness, goodness, faithfulness, 23 gentleness and self-control. Against such things there is no law. 24 Those who belong to Christ Jesus have crucified the sinful nature with its passions and desires. 25 Since we live by the Spirit, let us keep in step with the Spirit. 26 Let us not become conceited, provoking and envying each other.

EXPLORE Paul is writing to a young church in Asia Minor, explaining how legalism – the rigid adherence to a set of rules – is not the freedom Jesus came to give us. When we allow the Holy Spirit to direct our lives (v 16) then we will not want to act as we used to. In case you think this all happened a long time ago and we are more civilised now, look closely at Paul's catalogue of sinful behaviour (vs 19–21). Most of it is depressingly recognisable in our lives today! We need to be honest – such behaviour can still be part of our nature. But when we let the Holy Spirit lead us, qualities of a different sort become apparent: 'love, joy, peace, patience, kindness, goodness, faithfulness, gentleness and self-control'. Our relationships with each other will be guided by these characteristics rather than selfishness and aggression.

You probably don't know anyone who manifests all of the qualities of verses 22 and 23 all of the time. But look at Jesus! He shows all these attributes to perfection, and has sent his Holy Spirit to help us become like him. As we cooperate with the Spirit's leading and teaching, so these beautiful, fruitful qualities will develop in our lives.

RESPOND God wants you to show all the qualities of verses 22 and 23! Which one do you think you might find hardest? Ask God to help you especially with that fruit.

Day 28

How do I know what God wants?

PREPARE It isn't always easy to know what God wants us to do! We sometimes think it wou be very helpful if his voice thundered from the skies in answer to our prayers! But we need not wait for such thunder: God speaks to us in many ways. Think about things that you hav been praying for (look at your prayer journal, if you've been keeping one): what answers ha God already given you?

Proverbs 3:1–12

My son, do not forget my teaching,
  but keep my commands in your heart,
2 for they will prolong your life many years
  and bring you prosperity.
3 Let love and faithfulness never leave you;
  bind them around your neck,
  write them on the tablet of your heart.
4 Then you will win favour and a good name
  in the sight of God and man.
5 Trust in the LORD with all your heart
  and lean not on your own understanding;
6 in all your ways acknowledge him,
  and he will make your paths straight.
7 Do not be wise in your own eyes;
  fear the LORD and shun evil.
8 This will bring health to your body
  and nourishment to your bones.
9 Honour the LORD with your wealth,
  with the firstfruits of all your crops;
10 then your barns will be filled to overflowing,
  and your vats will brim over with new wine.
11 My son, do not despise the LORD's discipline
  and do not resent his rebuke,
12 because the LORD disciplines those he loves,
  as a father the son he delights in.

EXPLORE If we read and reflect on Goc word, and receive sound Christian teaching in our church fellowship, we will know what we should do in many situations (v 1). God's rules for good living as revealed in the Bible are very clear, and it should always be the first place we turn for guidance. As we rea it faithfully and prayerfully in God's presence, we can sense his voice speaking to us. However, if we are seeking guidance in a life-changing situation on which there is no obvious answer from biblical principles (e.g. 'Should I take job X or job Y?'), it is always a good idea to talk and pray about it with a mature Christian.

We all have an inbuilt tendency to fe that we know best (vs 5,7); all too oft when we say that we are seeking guidance, what we are really seeking i permission to be disobedient! When v respect and revere God, and submit to his loving commands (v 7), he provide a way through our problems (v 6). Perhaps you have already experienced God's help like this. If you have, tell others about it. It will encourage thos who are struggling with problems of their own, and strengthen your faith.

RESPOND 'Loving Father, please open my eyes and my ears to hear what you are saying to me; help me to order my own li according to your will not mine.'

Day 29

Shining in the darkness

PREPARE When we become a Christian, it isn't like joining a club, going along once a week nd quietly doing our own thing! Jesus calls us to stand out boldly, to be visible. Sounds a bit incomfortable? Thank God that he has sent his Holy Spirit to be with you.

Matthew 5:13–16

¹3 "You are the salt of the earth. But if the alt loses its saltiness, how can it be made alty again? It is no longer good for nything, except to be thrown out and rampled by men.

¹4 "You are the light of the world. A city n a hill cannot be hidden. ¹5 Neither do people light a lamp and put it under a bowl. Instead they put it on its stand, and t gives light to everyone in the house. ¹6 In the same way, let your light shine before men, that they may see your good leeds and praise your Father in heaven."

EXPLORE What do we use salt for today? In the ancient world it was used not just to add flavour, but as a preservative – vital in a hot climate before refrigeration! Jesus calls us to be salt: to preserve the good in society, to stop it 'going bad' – to make a difference. At the beginning of the twenty-first century, church leaders of all denominations are calling for a restoration of Christian values in society, to counteract the slide into moral degeneration. Often such calls have led to opposition and ridicule. But Jesus is – and always has been – calling us to be the preservers of moral standards, leading by example, regardless of society's reaction. If we do not we are valueless, like salt which no longer preserves (v 13). Going against what society finds acceptable or praiseworthy may put us in an uncomfortable position. We might feel that we have done enough if we make our views known then quietly fade into the background. But just as the lights of a hilltop town can be seen from far away at night, so we are called to be visible – guiding lights in our communities. It's no good being a shiny Christian at home and church if we then hide our light at work or with friends (v 15)! If what we do and believe as Christians is invisible, how will others know about God?

RESPOND Think: How do others know I am a Christian?

Day 30

Why go to church?

PREPARE No athlete expects to win an Olympic gold the first time they start running! Similarly, our Christian life will have plenty of ups and downs, successes and failures. But th is plenty of help along the way. Over the next eleven days we will discover some of the help God gives us to keep going. We all talk about 'going to church', and usually call the building itself 'the church'. But the building isn't *really* the church: we are! Before reading today's passage, think of all those Christians who have helped you in your Christian life, and thank God for their encouragement.

1 Corinthians 12:12–27

12 The body is a unit, though it is made up of many parts; ... So it is with Christ. 13 For we were all baptised by one Spirit into one body – whether Jews or Greeks, slave or free – and we were all given the one Spirit to drink.

14 Now the body is not made up of one part but of many. ... 16 And if the ear should say, "Because I am not an eye, I do not belong to the body," it would not for that reason cease to be part of the body. 17 If the whole body were an eye, where would the sense of hearing be? ... 18 But in fact God has arranged the parts in the body, every one of them, just as he wanted them to be. 19 If they were all one part, where would the body be? 20 As it is, there are many parts, but one body.

21 The eye cannot say to the hand, "I don't need you!" ... 22 On the contrary, those parts of the body that seem to be weaker are indispensable, 23 and the parts that we think are less honourable we treat with special honour. And the parts that are unpresentable are treated with special modesty, 24 while our presentable parts need no special treatment. ... 25 there should be no division in the body, but ... its parts should have equal concern for each other. 26 If one part suffers, every part suffers with it; if one part is honoured, every part rejoices with it.

27 Now you are the body of Christ, and each one of you is a part of it.

EXPLORE Have you ever hurt your thum and couldn't use it for a while? It probably stopped you performing ever ordinary tasks. Such a small part of ou body, but don't we notice it when it is out of action? Paul uses the picture of physical body to illustrate how the church functions. We are all part of th body (v 27) and we each need to play our different parts as God intends (v 1

The Corinthian church evidently thought some members were more important than others. Paul firmly squashes this idea: everyone is important. God has given us different responsibilities, all of them equally significant and all of them contributing equally to the health of the whole.

A part of the body that is detached cannot function, and the body is damaged by its absence. Our sore thu will not get better if it is amputated, a our hand will not work properly witho its thumb. We cannot say, 'I believe in Jesus, but I do not need to go to churc As believers we are part of his body. W need others, and they need us. We nee to be integrated into a fellowship of believers.

RESPOND Think: Are you a part of a chur – a fellowship of Christians? How could y become more involved?

Day 31

'I love you'

PREPARE Pray: 'Father, give me a greater understanding of your love.'
Today's passage is well known, and is often used as a reading at church wedding ceremonies. People get a little misty-eyed as they watch two people in love starting out as a married couple! But that's not really what the passage is about. See what you think, as you read it.

1 Corinthians 13

If I speak in the tongues of men and of angels, but have not love, I am only a resounding gong or a clanging cymbal. ² If I have the gift of prophecy and can fathom all mysteries and all knowledge, and if I have a faith that can move mountains, but have not love, I am nothing. ³ If I give all I possess to the poor and surrender my body to the flames, but have not love, I gain nothing.

⁴ Love is patient, love is kind. It does not envy, it does not boast, it is not proud. ⁵ It is not rude, it is not self-seeking, it is not easily angered, it keeps no record of wrongs. ⁶ Love does not delight in evil but rejoices with the truth. ⁷ It always protects, always trusts, always hopes, always perseveres.

⁸ Love never fails. But where there are prophecies, they will cease; where there are tongues, they will be stilled; where there is knowledge, it will pass away. ⁹ For we know in part and we prophesy in part, ¹⁰ but when perfection comes, the imperfect disappears. ¹¹ When I was a child, I talked like a child, I thought like a child, I reasoned like a child. When I became a man, I put childish ways behind me. ¹² Now we see but a poor reflection as in a mirror; then we shall see face to face. Now I know in part; then I shall know fully, even as I am fully known.

¹³ And now these three remain: faith, hope and love. But the greatest of these is love.

EXPLORE Paul is not talking here about when two people are in love. He is talking about the love Christians are to show to all others, whoever they are. This is the love Jesus spoke of when he told the disciples to 'love each other as I have loved you' (John 15:12) and to 'love your enemies' (Luke 6:27). (The Greek word for this kind of love is *agape*, and you may hear some Christians talk about 'agape love'.)

We have all met people, even in the caring professions, who do their work efficiently but without any warmth or real concern for others. If we try to serve God and our fellow men and women in the same way, our work is valueless (vs 1–3). Love is at the heart of the Christian faith: without it we are nothing (v 2). It is a love that forgives, and does not bear grudges or seek revenge. It is easy to think of a 'good life' as one that merely avoids doing wrong. But a truly good life goes deeper: it is one driven by love. Love is positive, enabling relationships to deepen in trust and commitment.

Love – Christ's love – will never fail. Nothing in this world is perfect, but our future with God, in eternity, will be gloriously perfect (vs 10,12). Hallelujah!

RESPOND Jesus loves you like this. How can you begin to show this love to others? Remember that you have the Holy Spirit to help you.

Day 32

A recipe for relationships

PREPARE Do you pray regularly for those in your church? It is a sad fact of Christian life tha there always seem to be divisions and arguments amongst Christians. Sometimes this even leads to splits within churches. Paul knows our human weaknesses and sins, and knows too how such divisions grieve God. His advice to the young Thessalonian church is just as appropriate for your church today.

1 Thessalonians 5:12–28

12 Now we ask you, brothers, to respect those who work hard among you, who are over you in the Lord and who admonish you. 13 Hold them in the highest regard in love because of their work. Live in peace with each other. 14 And we urge you, brothers, warn those who are idle, encourage the timid, help the weak, be patient with everyone. 15 Make sure that nobody pays back wrong for wrong, but always try to be kind to each other and to everyone else.

16 Be joyful always; 17 pray continually; 18 give thanks in all circumstances, for this is God's will for you in Christ Jesus.

19 Do not put out the Spirit's fire; 20 do not treat prophecies with contempt. 21 Test everything. Hold on to the good. 22 Avoid every kind of evil.

23 May God himself, the God of peace, sanctify you through and through. May your whole spirit, soul and body be kept blameless at the coming of our Lord Jesus Christ. 24 The one who calls you is faithful and he will do it.

25 Brothers, pray for us. 26 Greet all the brothers with a holy kiss. 27 I charge you before the Lord to have this letter read to all the brothers.

28 The grace of our Lord Jesus Christ be with you.

EXPLORE Paul's letter was read to all th church (v 27), and so is a message to of us. We are to respect, honour and love those set over us: gossiping and grumbling about the minister/vicar/ pastor/eldership/deacons/church- wardens are out (vs 12,13)! The same applies to our relationships with othe in the church (v 14). Revenge and retaliation are not even to be con- sidered (v 15). When you hear a bit o 'news' about someone, put it through sieve of three questions before even thinking about passing it on: 'Is it tru Is it kind? Is it necessary?' If it stops a any of these, it should go no further.

Our relationship with God is at the heart of our relationships with others. Prayer is our priority (v 17). Gathering to pray as a church is not an optional extra, but a vital part of fellowship.

God does not work according to ou preconceived ideas or plans. We need be prayerfully welcoming of anything that is of the Spirit (vs 19,20), at the same time asking for discernment (vs 21,22) to separate the good from evil Humanly speaking, all this might seen hard task, but Paul knows that becaus of the grace of God, we are able to liv together in peace (vs 23,24).

RESPOND Reflect on verses 16–18 (perha learning them or writing them out) and enjoy the friendship of other Christians!

Day 33

What are spiritual gifts?

PREPARE Think of all the things God has given you, and thank him for them. Like those gifts, spiritual gifts are presents to us from God our Father. They are not given to us in order to enhance our status, or show how much more God loves us than anyone else; they are given for us to use in the church to bring glory to God and show the power of Jesus. We cannot do anything to earn these gifts; God distributes them according to his wishes and his grace.

Romans 12:3–8

3 For by the grace given me I say to every one of you: Do not think of yourself more highly than you ought, but rather think of yourself with sober judgement, in accordance with the measure of faith God has given you. 4 Just as each of us has one body with many members, and these members do not all have the same function, 5 so in Christ we who are many form one body, and each member belongs to all the others. 6 We have different gifts, according to the grace given us. If a man's gift is prophesying, let him use it in proportion to his faith. 7 If it is serving, let him serve; if it is teaching, let him teach; 8 if it is encouraging, let him encourage; if it is contributing to the needs of others, let him give generously; if it is leadership, let him govern diligently; if it is showing mercy, let him do it cheerfully.

EXPLORE Here Paul urges us not to use God's gifts as status symbols. We all have a certain standard of faith (v 3); comparing our gifts with others' is pointless and shows a lack of humility. Paul mentions different types of gifts to use in the church (vs 6–8). In 1 Corinthians 12:1–11 (which we will be looking at tomorrow) he mentions some more; read that passage now to see what they are.

(Note: there is sometimes disagreement in the church about spiritual gifts. If the Bible readings and our notes for today and tomorrow leave you puzzled, please do talk to leaders or other wise Christians in your church about them.)

No gift from God is more important than another. They are all needed for the church to function as a coordinated body (vs 4,5). What is most important is that we use our gifts fully, for the good of all (vs 5–8). The 'speaking' gifts are perhaps the most obvious, and receive attention both inside and outside the church. The gifts of practical service, however, are vitally important in showing the love of Jesus to one another and to unbelievers. They may well have more impact – especially on those outside the church – than all the words spoken inside the church.

RESPOND Praise the Lord that we do not have to rely on our own abilities in order to serve him.

Day 34

A gift for me?

PREPARE After my grandparents died, we found some of their wedding presents from 60 years before, still in the wrapping paper. They had never used them. Do we treat God's gift to us like that?

1 Corinthians 12:1–11

Now about spiritual gifts, brothers, I do not want you to be ignorant. 2 You know that when you were pagans, somehow or other you were influenced and led astray to mute idols. 3 Therefore I tell you that no-one who is speaking by the Spirit of God says, "Jesus be cursed," and no-one can say, "Jesus is Lord," except by the Holy Spirit.

4 There are different kinds of gifts, but the same Spirit. 5 There are different kinds of service, but the same Lord. 6 There are different kinds of working, but the same God works all of them in all men.

7 Now to each one the manifestation of the Spirit is given for the common good. 8 To one there is given through the Spirit the message of wisdom, to another the message of knowledge by means of the same Spirit, 9 to another faith by the same Spirit, to another gifts of healing by that one Spirit, 10 to another miraculous powers, to another prophecy, to another distinguishing between spirits, to another speaking in different kinds of tongues, and to still another the interpretation of tongues. 11 All these are the work of one and the same Spirit, and he gives them to each one, just as he determines.

EXPLORE God's gifts to us are there to be used for the 'common good', not proudly or selfishly. And no one has been left off God's gift list! Paul refers to gifts, service and working (vs 4–6) – all different ways of bringing glory to God. They are to be used for 'the common good' – that is, to build up the church, encouraging, teaching and strengthening the faith of the believers, and demonstrating the power of God.

In first-century Corinth, as in Athens, the parading of abilities such as eloquent speech-making was much admired; and in the pagan temples, signs of power were expected. Paul denounces this attitude among Christians: perhaps the gifts he mentions in verses 8–10 were ones the Corinthians were boasting about and squabbling over which was the most important. What can we learn here?

First, Paul says that everyone has a gift (v 7); secondly, it is obvious that we don't have to be perfect to receive our gifts for God! The Corinthian Christians caused Paul a lot of heartache, and yet he has no doubt at all that they have God-given gifts – he is only anxious that they use them properly! How exciting to know that we are given spiritual gifts and we don't have to pass a test first!

RESPOND Pray that God will help you to recognise and use your gifts for his glory. You should talk and pray about this with other Christians in your church.

Day 35

Do this in remembrance of me

PREPARE Your own church may call it Holy Communion, Eucharist or The Lord's Supper. But whatever title you give it, at its heart lies the command of Jesus in today's passage to 'do this in remembrance of me'.

Luke 22:7–22

... 8 Jesus sent Peter and John, saying, "Go and make preparations for us to eat the Passover."

9 "Where do you want us to prepare for it?" they asked.

10 He replied, "As you enter the city, a man carrying a jar of water will meet you. Follow him to the house that he enters, 11 and say to the owner of the house, 'The Teacher asks: Where is the guest room, where I may eat the Passover with my disciples?' 12 He will show you a large upper room, all furnished. Make preparations there."

13 They left and found things just as Jesus had told them. So they prepared the Passover.

14 When the hour came, Jesus and his apostles reclined at the table. 15 And he said to them, "I have eagerly desired to eat this Passover with you before I suffer. 16 For I tell you, I will not eat it again until it finds fulfilment in the kingdom of God."

17 After taking the cup, he gave thanks and said, "Take this and divide it among you. 18 For I tell you I will not drink again of the fruit of the vine until the kingdom of God comes."

19 And he took bread, gave thanks and broke it, and gave it to them, saying, "This is my body given for you; do this in remembrance of me."

20 In the same way, after the supper he took the cup, saying, "This cup is the new covenant in my blood, which is poured out for you. 21 But the hand of him who is going to betray me is with mine on the table."

EXPLORE Jesus and his disciples are celebrating the Passover (the Feast of Unleavened Bread) commemorating the deliverance of the Israelites out of Egypt and slavery. But Jesus takes this Passover meal and makes it into something new. As he breaks the unleavened bread he likens it to his own body, which will be broken and tortured for our deliverance from punishment for our sins (v 19). He likens the wine to his blood, which will flow from his crucified body, as a sacrifice on our behalf (v 20). The new covenant – that is, the new agreement God makes with us for forgiveness of our sin – has been confirmed, not by animal sacrifices, but by the body and blood of Jesus himself.

We celebrate the meal as a group of believers, united in the love of Christ. In the earliest account we have of such a meal (1 Corinthians 11:17–34) it is obvious that the Lord's Supper is meant to be a solemn and reverent occasion. As we take the bread and the wine, we are remembering what Jesus has done for each one of us who believes. As you hold the bread, feel the rough edges and remember how Jesus' body was flogged raw and nails driven through his hands and feet. As you drink the wine, look into its redness and think of the blood that flowed from his wounds.

RESPOND 'How can I thank you enough, Lord, for loving me so much that you died for me?'

Day 36

Knowing the enemy

PREPARE It is very difficult to fight a war if you don't know who the enemy is. Sudden atta take us completely unawares. The devil is our enemy. Today he is most often seen as a comi figure, with horns and a tail, and even Christians can be unaware of both his existence and schemes. But he does exist, and is a powerful – although defeated – enemy.

Matthew 4:1–11

Then Jesus was led by the Spirit into the desert to be tempted by the devil. 2 After fasting for forty days and forty nights, he was hungry. 3 The tempter came to him and said, "If you are the Son of God, tell these stones to become bread."

4 Jesus answered, "It is written: 'Man does not live on bread alone, but on every word that comes from the mouth of God.'"

5 Then the devil took him to the holy city and had him stand on the highest point of the temple. 6 "If you are the Son of God," he said, "throw yourself down. For it is written:

" 'He will command his angels concern-
    ing you,
  and they will lift you up in their hands,
so that you will not strike your foot
    against a stone.'"

7 Jesus answered him, "It is also written: 'Do not put the Lord your God to the test.'"

8 Again, the devil took him to a very high mountain and showed him all the kingdoms of the world and their splendour. 9 "All this I will give you," he said, "if you will bow down and worship me."

10 Jesus said to him, "Away from me, Satan! For it is written: 'Worship the Lord your God, and serve him only.'"

11 Then the devil left him, and angels came and attended him.

EXPLORE The devil is a dirty fighter, an often attacks us when we are weak an vulnerable (v 2). His methods are underhand, and appeal to our individ weaknesses. Jesus was without sin, bu he was human and the devil tries to tempt him, just as he will tempt us.

The devil's first ploy is to try to get Jesus to use his power for his own end (v 3). Food would have been more th welcome – but we must rely on God, not ourselves. Jesus defeats him, as we can, by using God's Word (v 4). The devil, who knows the Bible far better than we do, turns this round and says 'OK then, God says he will protect you go on, jump from this great height' (v 6). Jesus sees through this; if we trust and love someone, there is no need to put them to a test (v 7). So the devil appeals to pride and desire for power, offering an easy way out of the death Jesus knows he will have to suffer (vs 8,9). And he says exactly the same to offering us 'the easy way out' – the ea life we can live if we ignore God's will

Sadly, many succumb to the devil's schemes. But we have the same resources to defend ourselves and bea the devil as Jesus did, and tomorrow w will read more about them.

RESPOND Think about, and perhaps memorise, these words: 'Worship the Lor your God, and serve him only' (v 10).

Day 37

Our defences are up!

PREPARE Reflect: 'The Lord is my strength and my shield; my heart trusts in him, and I am helped' (Psalm 28:7).
Although the devil is real and does attack us, we have impregnable defences available to us.

Ephesians 6:10–18

¹⁰ Finally, be strong in the Lord and in his mighty power. ¹¹ Put on the full armour of God so that you can take your stand against the devil's schemes. ¹² For our struggle is not against flesh and blood, but against the rulers, against the authorities, against the powers of this dark world and against the spiritual forces of evil in the heavenly realms. ¹³ Therefore put on the full armour of God, so that when the day of evil comes, you may be able to stand your ground, and after you have done everything, to stand. ¹⁴ Stand firm then, with the belt of truth buckled round your waist, with the breastplate of righteousness in place, ¹⁵ and with your feet fitted with the readiness that comes from the gospel of peace. ¹⁶ In addition to all this, take up the shield of faith, with which you can extinguish all the flaming arrows of the evil one. ¹⁷ Take the helmet of salvation and the sword of the Spirit, which is the word of God. ¹⁸ And pray in the Spirit on all occasions with all kinds of prayers and requests. With this in mind, be alert and always keep on praying for all the saints.

EXPLORE Paul is well aware that the devil uses dirty tricks to undermine our faith (v 11); but he also knows that God has given us the means of defending ourselves. He uses the picture of a Roman soldier clad in belt, breastplate (v 14) and stout footwear (v 15), with a shield (v 16), helmet and sword (v 17), to describe the armour God has given us. Just like the Roman soldier, we need *all* the armour. Think about how you would get hurt if you left a bit off. But that 'belt of truth' is crucial. Truth is an essential part of our Christian lives. Experiences and warm feelings are not enough: we need to know the truth of God's Word, knowing that God loves us and that our sins are forgiven – and then live lives which reflect that truth. Paul tells us to 'stand firm' (v 14), and we can defend ourselves in the same way that Jesus defended himself from the devil: with truth, righteousness, a living relationship with our Father, and the Word of God. If you know God's Word you know the truth, and know that what the devil says, however attractive it may seem, is lies. Finally, it's important to keep praying (v 18).

In all dirty wars, enemies never give up. The devil's final defeat is still to come, when Jesus returns in glory and power. We need to keep on the alert.

RESPOND A verse to think about and perhaps memorise: 'If God is for us, who can be against us?' (Romans 8:31).

Day 38

Jesus will come again

PREPARE Jesus promised his disciples that he would come to earth again, and some of the first Christians believed that this would happen in their lifetime. But nearly two thousand years have gone by, and still Jesus hasn't come back. Is he really going to come again?

Matthew 24:23–41

23 "... if anyone says to you, 'Look, here is the Christ!' ... do not believe it. 24 For false Christs and false prophets will appear and perform great signs and miracles to deceive even the elect ... 26 So if anyone tells you, 'There he is, out in the desert,' do not go out; or, 'Here he is, in the inner rooms,' do not believe it. 27 For as lightning that comes from the east is visible even in the west, so will be the coming of the Son of Man. ...

29 "Immediately after the distress of those days

"'the sun will be darkened,
   and the moon will not give its light;
the stars will fall from the sky,
   and the heavenly bodies will be shaken.'

30 "At that time the sign of the Son of Man will appear in the sky ... They will see the Son of Man coming on the clouds of the sky, with power and great glory. 31 And ... his angels ... will gather his elect from the four winds, from one end of the heavens to the other.

32 "Now learn this lesson from the fig-tree: As soon as its ... leaves come out, you know that summer is near. 33 Even so, when you see all these things, you know that it is near, right at the door. 34 I tell you the truth, this generation will certainly not pass away until all these things have happened. 35 Heaven and earth will pass away, but my words will never pass away.

36 "No-one knows about that day or hour, not even the angels in heaven, nor the Son, but only the Father ..."

EXPLORE The world is not going to e with a whimper, but with cataclysmic cosmic events (v 29), and Jesus will come again (v 30). He said he would he will. This time, however, he will n come as a humble servant, but in all power and glory to gather up all Christians to be with him (vs 30,31). Many self-styled 'prophets' have, ove the centuries, forecast the end of the world based on their interpretations this and other passages in the Bible. even Jesus didn't know when the end would come (v 36). What *is* certain is that it will come suddenly (vs 27,38,3 We must be prepared for that day, keeping to the true faith.

Jesus knows that many will claim t the returning Christ (or 'Messiah'), th many who say they are sent by God perform miracles and supernatural a which could deceive Christians (vs 23 24). Today, as in the past, we see the growth of false cults, often claiming be the true church and led by men w call themselves, or are seen as, a Messiah. Only by knowing the truth what the Bible tells us, and constant reminding ourselves of that truth, wi we be able to live for God and stand against lies and deceptions, and be ready for Jesus when he comes again

RESPOND Reflect on some of the promis that God as given you in the passages of the Bible which you have read over the few weeks.

Day 39

He will judge the earth

PREPARE Pray: 'Teach me your truth, Lord, as I read your Word today.'
When Jesus, the Son of God, comes again in supernatural power and awesome glory, he will come as judge of all the earth. Unbelievers are going to receive a great shock!

Matthew 13:24–30,36–43

24 Jesus told them another parable: "The kingdom of heaven is like a man who sowed good seed in his field. 25 But while everyone was sleeping, his enemy came and sowed weeds among the wheat ... 26 When the wheat sprouted ... then the weeds also appeared.

27 "The owner's servants ... said, 'Sir ... where ... did the weeds come from?'

28 "'An enemy did this,' he replied.

"The servants asked him, 'Do you want us to go and pull them up?'

29 "'No,' he answered, ... 30 "Let both grow together until the harvest. ... I will tell the harvesters: First collect the weeds and tie them in bundles to be burned; then gather the wheat and bring it into my barn." ...

. His disciples came to him and said, "Explain to us the parable of the weeds in the field."

37 He answered, "The one who sowed the good seed is the Son of Man. 38 The field is the world, and the good seed ... the sons of the kingdom. The weeds are the sons of the evil one, 39 and the enemy who sows them is the devil. The harvest is the end of the age, and the harvesters are angels.

40 "As the weeds are pulled up and burned in the fire, so it will be at the end of the age. 41 The Son of Man will send out his angels, and they will weed out of his kingdom everything that causes sin and all who do evil. 42 They will throw them into the fiery furnace, where there will be weeping and gnashing of teeth. 43 Then the righteous will shine like the sun in the kingdom of their Father ..."

EXPLORE The weeds Jesus talks about are probably darnel grass – a grass that looks exactly like good wheat in its early stages. Only later can the difference be seen, by which time the roots are so intertwined that to uproot the darnel grass would destroy the wheat (v 29). Christians live closely among those who are not Christians, and our lives are inevitably affected by them. It can be discouraging to see how many people seem to get away with the wicked things they do, and often we wish that they would get their just desserts now. But justice *will* be done. When Jesus comes to judge the earth, all those who are not God's children will be uprooted and destroyed (vs 41,42), while those who believe in Jesus and live God's way will be taken to be with their Father (v 43).

There is judgement for all of us, for not one of us is innocent of sin, and we all have to give an account even for every careless word we have spoken (Matthew 12:36). But for those who believe, there is only rejoicing, because our accounts with God have been settled by Jesus.

We read yesterday that we do not know when Jesus will come again – but whenever it is, we need to be ready and rejoicing. A glorious welcome awaits us in our Father's kingdom.

RESPOND Think about your own life. Think about being with God for eternity, and thank him that Jesus has made this possible.

Day 40

Keeping going

PREPARE **Pray: 'Father God, I want to go your way. Help me to follow your guidance.'**
Sometimes life is jogging along in a fairly comfortable way, when 'Whoomph!' – we seem
come up against one of those army-type assault courses. We just manage to struggle over
obstacle, to find that there's another, even worse, on the other side. Paul knows that life c
be like that, even for Christians.

2 Timothy 2:1–13

You then, my son, be strong in the grace that is in Christ Jesus. 2 And the things you have heard me say in the presence of many witnesses entrust to reliable men who will also be qualified to teach others. 3 Endure hardship with us like a good soldier of Christ Jesus. 4 No-one serving as a soldier gets involved in civilian affairs – he wants to please his commanding officer.
5 Similarly, if anyone competes as an athlete, he does not receive the victor's crown unless he competes according to the rules. 6 The hardworking farmer should be the first to receive a share of the crops.
7 Reflect on what I am saying, for the Lord will give you insight into all this.

8 Remember Jesus Christ, raised from the dead, descended from David. This is my gospel, 9 for which I am suffering even to the point of being chained like a criminal. But God's word is not chained. 10 Therefore I endure everything for the sake of the elect, that they too may obtain the salvation that is in Christ Jesus, with eternal glory.

11 Here is a trustworthy saying:

If we died with him,
  we will also live with him;
12 if we endure,
  we will also reign with him.
If we disown him,
  he will also disown us;
13 if we are faithless,
  he will remain faithful,
  for he cannot disown himself.

EXPLORE 'Be strong' says Paul to Timothy, who seemed to be rather timid, needing a lot of encourageme Like some of us, really! Paul is saying that Timothy doesn't have to worry about his own abilities: because of G grace, his strength lies in Jesus (v 1). The same is true for us: this strength from God will get us through all that throws at us. Of course, we need to I single-minded about following Jesus 4), and lovingly obey God's comman (v 5); life is not going to be easy, but will get our reward (v 6). Life may se puzzling, and God may sometimes fe distant, but when we think and pray, the Spirit will make things clear (v 7)

The last three verses, from a very e Christian hymn, encourage us throug all difficulties. God is always faithful, however faithless we are, because his very nature is faithfulness. He will ne let us down, and his words are alway true. However hard we find life, God always there to help us. He is not bawling from the sidelines like a sergeant-major, urging 'Get a move but is with us at every difficulty, sayin 'Put your trust in me; go my way, it's best way. We'll get there safely.'

What next?

We hope that *Daily Bread for New Christians* has helped to get you into the habit of reading the Bible regularly. Look again at the note for Day 21 to remind yourself of the importance of the Bible in a Christian's life. Now that you've finished these notes, you may be wondering, 'What next?'. We want to encourage you to keep on reading the Bible and meeting God in his Word. Why not take a look at *Daily Bread*? It's written in the same style as *Daily Bread for New Christians*, containing encouragement, inspiration and practical help for every day.

Talk to mature Christian friends to find out what helps them to meet God through reading the Bible. If you have a local Christian bookshop, you will find a wide variety of publications there to help you read the Bible regularly and meaningfully. These include Bible reading guides, most of which have a reading for each day. Scripture Union produces plenty of material to help adults (and children) meet God in the Bible; to read some information on the Bible reading guides we produce for adults take a look at the inside back cover.

Title	Quantity	UK	Europe	Rest of world
Daily Bread		£15.00	£20.00	£23.00
Closer to God		£15.00	£20.00	£23.00
Encounter with God		£15.80	£20.00	£23.00
	Total			

Payment details

Subscription	£
Gifts to Scripture Union's evangelistic work	£
BRGs total (see below) £	**I enclose total payment of** £

___ by Postal Order or by cheque payable to Scripture Union

___ or please debit my credit/debit card: Security code | | | |

Card No | | | | | | | | | | | | | | | |

Expiry Date | | | | Issue No (Switch only) | | | Valid from | | | |

Name on card

Cardholder's signature Date

or tick here ⬤ **to pay annually by Direct Debit (ring 0845 07 06 006 for details)**

ORNCa

Personal details

Mr/Mrs/Miss/Rev/Other Name

Address

Postcode

Email Daytime tel

* Please enter total price of Bible reading guides ordered in **BRGs total** section in upper part of form.

Subtotal	£
P&P	£
BRGs total *	**£**

Postage & Packing costs

Order Value	UK	Europe	Rest of world
Under £7.00	£1.50	£2.50	£3.50
£7.00 to £11.99	£2.50	£3.75	£5.50
£12.00 to £24.99	Free	£5.00	£7.50
£25.00 and over	Free	20% of value	30% of value

You can place your orders:
· Through your local Christian bookshop · By phone 0845 07 06 006 · Online: www.scriptureunion.org.uk
· By post: Scripture Union, Mail Order, PO Box 5148, Milton Keynes MLO, MK2 2YX